Mistakes Are Your Capital

Mistakes Are Your Capital

Turn Entrepreneurial Errors into Business Opportunities

Jay J. Silverberg

Mistakes Are Your Capital:
Turn Entrepreneurial Errors into Business Opportunities

Cover design by Charlene Kronstedt

Interior design by S4Carlisle Publishing Services, Chennai, India

First published in 2026 by
Business Expert Press, LLC
222 East 46th Street, New York, NY 10017
www.businessexpertpress.com

ISBN-13: 978-1-60649-571-1 (paperback)
ISBN-13: 978-1-60649-587-2 (e-book)

Entrepreneurship and Small Business Management Collection

First edition: 2026

10 9 8 7 6 5 4 3 2 1

EU SAFETY REPRESENTATIVE
Mare Nostrum Group B.V.
Doelen 72
4831 GR Breda
The Netherlands
gpsr@mare-nostrum.co.uk

"Experience is the name everyone gives to their mistakes."
—Oscar Wilde

"Making mistakes isn't enough to become great. You must also admit the mistake and then learn how to turn that mistake into an advantage."
—Robert T. Kiyosaki

"The only real mistake is the one from which we learn nothing."
—John Powell

Introduction

It's not easy being human. We all mess up.

Mistakes ground us, especially those "in your face" missteps that stare you down. In business, stumbles have price tags, but there's a positive side. We can learn from the scalding of our entrepreneurial egos.

Mistakes Are Your Capital provides entrepreneurs, business managers, mentors, and educators with an innovative toolbox to identify, analyze, catalog, and categorize the seriousness and potential damages of business lapses, and, wherever feasible, plan remedial action that can create opportunities.

Admitting to mistakes is the **first step**. Coming up with strategies to deal with the ensuing obstacles and issues created rather than deflecting blame or finger-pointing is **step two**. Implementing those "move forward" tactics is **step three**. Learning from the gaffes to assure they don't repeat and bite us again, or even recognizing opportunities created by the missteps is **step four**. Only then can we proudly state that **mistakes are our capital.**

We are better for it.

In the process we foster solidarity and collaboration with our team and help create a more workable, trusting, and resilient environment that may cultivate a crew that is more fearless and innovative in delivering their responsibilities and projects, and generating greater value for the business.

We tend to dwell on our business successes and tell endless stories and exploits of ourselves as innovative, gifted, and daring entrepreneurs. Of course. Who wants to be reminded of those darker fumble-ridden experiences? Nobody really does.

Big mistake.

The cliche is "learn from your mistakes." But we often do not take that rule of thumb seriously. It is our survival instinct to selectively remember the good times, the entrepreneurial coups, and allow our minds, and our often-fragile self-esteem, to back-burner the hiccups. The failures.

But these nontriumphs also represent incredible learning experiences and opportunities.

This book is about business mistakes; what they are, how to recognize them, how to embrace them, how to avoid them wherever possible, and how to conceivably capitalize on them. Turn them into opportunities.

Mistakes are the teachers. They strengthen your skills, build confidence, hone your decision making and judgment calls, instill future error-avoidance, control your business journey, and steer the very pathway and direction of your venture.

How you learn and grow from your slipups represent the core of your business wealth. Your capital. The essence of your entrepreneurship.

Mistakes Are Your Capital is an assemblage of common (and some uncommon) blunders often made by businesspeople.

Many of the incidents in this book and the solutions/lessons learned have been gleaned from my mentoring and teaching a multitude of entrepreneurs and managers over the course of five decades. I have learned from miscues I have witnessed along the way, and I too have personally confronted some of the incidents highlighted in this book.

Good or bad, everything has consequences.

Collectively, from launching my dreadful Russian beer ("Russkie Brewskie"), to a multinational client unwittingly introducing a line of radioactive all-natural diapers, these host of snafus, many or most of which were reshaped into new and exciting opportunities (except the radioactive diaper product line).

The numerous real-world stories contained in this book are both insightful and entertaining, especially when viewed in hindsight, and often tend to shout "of course, why didn't I/we/you think of that?"

And as you take ownership of some of the entrepreneurial "faux pas" scenarios in this book, and you likely will, take comfort in knowing that you are not alone, and that most mistakes are salvageable or fixable, and were even necessary to divert you toward the right trajectory.

The lapses themselves, and understanding their causes, impact on you and your business, and taking decisive action for their ultimate resolution, provides the entrepreneur with a valuable remediation toolkit, and, more importantly, often represents the stepping stone for change and growth.

That's the core purpose of this book *Mistakes Are Your Capital,* and I am proud to be your seasoned tour guide.

What Inspired This Book

"A lesson learned is a lesson worth sharing"
—Wyatt Hendrie

Retrospection.

My first business venture, albeit at a young age, was digging for worms at midnight on the local golf course. The assumption was that bait for sports fishing was worth more than the costliest filet mignon.

I put a crew together, outfitted each with garden tools and bait buckets, and assembled everyone under the cover of darkness, with dusk being the best time to catch worms, at our neighborhood golf course.

I had already presold my entire worm catch to the local fishing supply and bait shop, and was already daydreaming about spending my earnings, picturing sheep loaded down with moneybags jumping over the fence, but, in this case, it was smiling worms.

It was an exciting venture, but, despite the best of intentions and marginal planning, I fell asleep under a tree at the first hole, and woke to find my crew dispersed, and my presence discovered by an angry groundskeeper.

My parents were angry at me, but proud. It was a mixed reaction.

I learned about the need for better planning and not simply focusing on spending my unrealized profits. **There was a need to do the work before claiming the prize.** An invaluable lesson for my future entrepreneurial undertakings and learned at 12 years old.

Planning yields performance.

My mistakes were my capital.

Contents

CHAPTER 1

Theme of This Book

"Right from the start, see yourself as running a business instead of being self-employed."

—The Myth Revisited. Michael Gerber

Mistakes Are Your Capital is built on a foundation of **eight fundamental truths**.

1. Mistakes are the hiccups you encounter and deal with as you journey along the Yellow Brick Road of business. Failure is giving up and walking away. That is a massive distinction. **This book does not advocate failure as a solution to deal with your business stumbles.**
2. Perfection in business is a time-consuming mindset fraught with the likelihood of creating false steps, real or simply perceived. A far more useful outlook is **"better but not best."** In most circumstances, **good enough is, well, good enough**.
3. The third premise is "comfort." The more comfortable you are, the less stigma you will experience when faced with blunders that have been made by yourself or your team. The less knee jerk your solutions will be.
4. Confidence is a close relative to comfort. It serves you well when faced with remedial decisions demanded when mistakes arise. An easy-going and self-assured outlook affords you more objectivity in identifying and implementing solutions.
5. **Business gaffes demand action**. They are often unwelcome but need to be embraced.
6. **Learning from adversity** is what helps take the fear out of subsequent failures and missteps or trying something new.

7. There is a classification of mistakes best referred to as "hidden," eclipsed by your personality, your way of conducting business or your values and scruples. They may be oblivious to you, but not so to those around you, your staff or your customers. They may require attention as well. Stay alert.
8. Mistakes are usually stepping stones for opportunities. They create change, which begets growth, which is a precursor to success. Mistakes truly are your capital.

Understand and accept these eight truisms and you will undoubtedly develop a greater, less stressful, and easier pathway to success.

Appreciating these foundational maxims will also help you welcome and endorse the host of counsel offered up in this book.

Most existing "business mistake" books, blogs, and YouTube videos are, in some form, generic training materials on improving readers' decision-making and management skills, and how to cope with business stumbles, many of which are often cited in very broad terms. Interesting, but band-aid solutions at best.

This book intentionally avoids generic advice such as "be a better planner" or "make smarter management decisions." This nebulous oft-cited advice offers little to comfort the entrepreneur. Mistakes are therefore often repeated.

Every real business case study depicted throughout this book also includes an expected outcome and a lesson to be learned, all of which represents invaluable insight and guidance for the reader.

This exemplifies my theme for this book, and for you.

Time to get started.

SECTION ONE

Defining, Understanding, and Capitalizing on Business Mistakes

Business mistakes take on many disguises. Some are subtle, while others rush toward you like a fire engine.

The one truth they all share is, as much as they impact you, they also provide an opportunity to learn how to cope and correct, the opportunity to better yourself as a businessperson, and the opportunity to capitalize on new possibilities and direction.

Mistakes Are Your Capital **encapsulates mistakes (or blunders, errors, miscues, missteps, or whatever handle you choose to apply), and emphasizes what they teach us, and how they build our personal character and professional capital, and future success.**

Business mistakes are your adversary, while at the same time, they can be used for your benefit.

From defining good, bad, and ugly mistakes and quantifying mistakes, to offering up novel definitions such as "failing upwards." Section ONE sets the stage toward understanding, dealing with, and engaging with mistakes, and winning.

CHAPTER 2

Good, Bad, and Ugly Mistakes

"Anyone who has never made a mistake has never tried anything new."
—Albert Einstein

If your business is "off the rails" or being impacted by any number of jolts and tempests, then it is likely the contributing mistakes fall within three principal categories: good, bad, and ugly.

Good Mistakes, by Definition

Business blunders that have some semblance or features of a workable foundation can lead to opportunities.

Good business mistakes teach valuable lessons, and the stumbles themselves do not have unresolvable destructive elements. They are generally not repeated. Ever.

They tend to be forward-thinking and have an inherent ability to be rekindled into worthwhile action that can be leveraged by the company to generate a return, or a reduction of operating costs. The outcomes can include new products or services, refocused strategies for growth or change, branding/marketing ideas, or adopting new market strategies.

Good business mistakes yield definable, quantifiable results.

Bad Mistakes

Bad mistakes range from being fixable to almost self-destructive, and can often include launching products or services that go nowhere, generally after insufficient market research and groundwork, spending money on expenses or assets that do not add value to the business, accumulating too much inventory in anticipation of a rush demand, or based on a whim, hiring a square cog who will likely never assimilate into your existing team, or, as is too common, delaying to make tough decisions.

Bad snafus have an impact that are generally felt over time. Even when corrected, their history tends to linger and are often brought up as "remember when" hurtful examples.

Finally, the Ugly Mistakes

These can be "business killers." In an unforgiving marketplace, it is often tough for the company to recover fully.

Ugly misjudgments could create market share losses, cash flow crises, declining customer support, wavering investor or stockholder support, damaged reputation or even legal action that creates liabilities (sometimes even terminal) and risks for the business. Any and all of which can delay or impede business rehabilitation.

Ugly mistakes have one saving grace; you will likely NOT repeat them, or possibly never have the opportunity to even do so.

Employing a "Mistakes Outcome and Impact Chart"

Mistakes can be rated using two features. The intention is to assign a "rating" for each of the many real-world stories or experiences written about in this book so as to offer the reader a clear understanding of the scope of the mistake and what the repercussions, good, bad, or ugly, might have been. How do these ratings work? What do they represent?

The following defines the "**Mistakes Outcome and Impact Chart.**"

a. The **severity score** of the blunder. Ratings go from a significant mistake (rated as "3") down to milder misstep (rated as "1") and,
b. the **nature and fixability** of the mistake are further detailed under one of the three columns, i.e., good, bad, or ugly mistakes.

For example, a "Good Mistake" rated as 2 is generally eminently fixable. At the opposite extreme, an "Ugly Mistake" rated as 3 represents a good time for you to seek out alternate business opportunities.

Score	Good Mistake Rating	Bad Mistake Rating	Ugly Mistake Rating
3	This good mistake uncovers and offers up a direct pathway to opportunities not currently part of the company's products or services, or institutes a change in the business's mindset or performance.	Fixable, but almost overwhelming. Demands your time and focus to consider and plan any remedial action.	Potentially catastrophic and requires immediate attention. Impact can alter the course of the venture. This includes mistakes by misjudgment, haste, greed or because of aggressive expectations, as example aggravating causes.
2	This good mistake causes only limited damage and can be contained and absorbed. It also represents a distinct learning experience for the company.	Serious, but was likely expected based on events such as competition, changing technologies, etc. Possibly requires a shift in your game plan.	Fallout from the mistake is evident and quantifiable but not fatal. Remediation will take time, and the business will likely recover, but incur financial and/or market share/and reputation costs.
1	Any damage incurred may inflict residual impact. It has been dealt with swiftly and the resulting lessons learned become part of the company's operational toolbox.	Can likely be back-burnered, but not forever. To be dealt with as time permits, or possibly delegated.	Not currently pressing but can create major issues if not dealt with in very short order. Should be tabled for action in the nearest term possible.

As part of the ratings package, there is also a **Lesson(s) Learned** text box that highlights what insight the experience may have yielded, how and why the good/bad/ugly scoring was arrived at, and what the reader can take away from the event.

Lesson(s) Learned: The results and impact of the mistakes, be they good, bad or ugly, will be discussed here. It is of paramount importance that each story delivers a message that the entrepreneur can take away from the incident. This insight is part of a useful toolbox for entrepreneurs as they hone their decision-making abilities.

How did the real-world experience/story presented in this chapter earn the authors' assigned rating in the "Mistake Outcome and Impact Chart"? This will be explained in italics in the Lesson(s) Learned box. Feel free to question and rethink the designated ratings. After all, that is part of the learning process and your own perception of "good/bad/ugly" business mistakes.

In my university days, our Advanced Business 401 professor asked each of us to develop an innovative business idea and present the Business Plan to the incoming student body to demonstrate the spirit of entrepreneurship.

I drew on American Civil War history. At that time there were mobile communities, often referred to as "Hell on Wheels," that shadowed union armies from one encampment to the next, delivering essential "services" for the soldiers. These included all the vices, including saloon parlors, and brothels.

I was dubiously inspired.

My business venture was to be called "Delish" (pseudonym) and it was to be a full-service cathouse. Painted bright red, my RVs were intended to follow the routes of the mobile food canteens as they serviced construction sites, office complex parking lots, government buildings, and other locations where groups congregated on breaks and lunch.

The concept was unique, and, as is often the case, this begs the question as to why nobody else was doing it. I didn't care. My business fantasy was unfolding.

The financial projections were awesome, with an expected EBITDA (earnings before interest, taxes, depreciation or amortization) of over 45 percent. A marketing campaign, albeit subdued, was laid out in my Marketing Plan. I even recall having discussions with a "pro" as a potential spokesmodel, Collette, a stage performer whose claim to fame was her fortitude and stamina.

By today's social standards, this project would be abhorrent. But, back then, it was titillating.

My classmates loved it, but, ultimately, Delish was shot down because of practical considerations; legal and licensing, location permits, insufficient market research, no focus group feedback sessions, resistance from the food truck merchant groups, wary funders, and a professor who considered Playboy's Hugh Hefner as the devil incarnate. My entrepreneurial enthusiasm had blinded me. Rose-colored glasses had prevailed.

My proposed venture was innovative, but impractical and unrealizable. All things considered, it was a bad idea fraught with mistakes in logic and implementation roadblocks. But, as with many flawed concepts, this exercise did give birth to a different workable model.

In actual fact, Delish eventually did make it to the marketplace as a high-end foodie and dessert truck, still bright red, and staffed with beautiful baristas. The products all had suggestive names and served up specialty coffees and decadent French pastries.

So, here we have a bad business that was originally built on a flimsy foundation, having made critical mistakes in market research and planning, and was faulty in its core direction. But, having gone the route of trying, it succeeded in undergoing a rebirth.

Mistakes were the business's stepping stones to opportunity.

Delish morphed into a workable venture, still innovative, that serviced a marketplace keen to partake in better food and drink than the meager offerings of competitor mobile food canteens. And the gorgeous baristas didn't hurt either.

It worked. Mistakes were Delish's capital.

The ratings chart for the "Delish" initiative would be as follows.

Score	Good Mistake Rating	Bad Mistake Rating	Ugly Mistake Rating
3			
2			
1			

Lesson(s) Learned: What started out as a quirky business concept quickly delivered a lesson that business is governed by host of parameters, constraints and roadblocks, many of which are unbreachable. Market research and step-by-step planning are crucial, and new milestones need to be set as each obstruction is eliminated. Further, Delish also demonstrated that almost any idea has some merit, possibly buried in a faulty business model, but ultimately bearing some value. A business model should rarely be set in concrete during its planning and development stages.

A somewhat outlandish idea became the foundation for a doable business opportunity that proved successful. The original concept became the pathway for an initiative not originally part of the proposal. A rating of "3" in the "Good Mistake Rating" is applicable.

CHAPTER 3

"Failing Forward" Should Really Be "Failing Upwards"

> *"Do not judge me by my successes, judge me by how many times I fell down and got back up again."*
>
> —Nelson Mandela

Failing Forward implies eliminating the paralysis brought about by fear of failure and using your newfound confidence and positive mindset to get back on track. **Moving forward follows closely after failure.**

> *"Sometimes, good things fall apart so better things could fall together."*
>
> —Marilyn Monroe.

Failing Upwards means never giving up, continuing to take risks, albeit more calculated ones, and working to succeed in whatever venture or undertaking you have a passion to pursue with a newfound strength, self-assurance, and steadfast determination that only surviving business mishaps and malaise can instill. Success is the only option.

> *"Failure is simply the opportunity to begin again, this time more intelligently."*
>
> —Henry Ford.

This book, *Mistakes Are Your Capital*, deals with a multitude of mistakes as they occur in virtually every aspect of business, what they are, how they got there, how to fix them, and how to "fail upwards" from each as a learning experience.

Those very mistakes become capital benefiting both you and your company.

Key "Fail Upwards" Prime Directives

- Every setback is a learning experience, a promise you make to adapt, an invitation to do better, and a bridge towards bigger and better opportunities.
- Don't be paralyzed by fear of failure. This is a natural "fear or flight" instinct that you need to control and not let it control you.
- Take time to understand what you have done and how you might react differently the next time.
- Mistakes and blunders can draw you into a deep chasm. Knowing this pending danger in advance will help you circumvent any mindset traps.
- Lessons learned from errors are investments in resilience.
- Failing is not a limitation. **"Failing Upwards" implies learning to believe in yourself, your judgment and your abilities, and moving onwards and upwards.**
- Anyone who does not make mistakes in business is a dormant overcautious entrepreneur rather than a proactive, success-oriented player.
- Innovation is often fueled by being fearless, but not to the point of being reckless.
- Nothing will ever be perfect. Count on imperfection.
- Learn to accept better and not necessarily best.
- A mistake may be an error in judgment but should not be taken as an error in character.
- Mistakes should not be perceived as a defeat, but as a necessary stage of building a business.
- Do not repeat mistakes, but do not stop taking calculated risks. Risk is the fodder that promotes growth.
- Past missteps are just that. The past. Reliving them and guilting yourself over and over blinds you to what prospects lie ahead.
- That having been said, those who understand the effort it takes to move beyond business blunders and failures are best suited to achieve success.

Nobody could express "Failing Upwards" better than in Winnie the Pooh.

"Do you see, Pooh? Do you see, Piglet?
Brains first and then Hard Work. Look at it!
That's the way to build a house," said Eeyore proudly.
The House at Pooh Corner, by A. A. Milne.

Fitting into the Japanese Consumer marketplace can be tricky. A multinational home appliance manufacturer was interested in launching their devices in the Japanese marketplace. The company was Eastern U.S. based, and had little understanding of the Japanese market, except the market reports that spoke of a growing demand for U.S. branded portable home appliances.

After a beta test launch carried out by the company produced mediocre results, our firm was hired to research the market and offer recommendations on how they might proceed. Our findings were most conclusive, and we suggested the following: design a unit that was more compact and suitable for the smaller homes and apartments in Japan; brand the product with larger company logos more desirous in this brand-crazed environment and increase the selling price. Products with higher prices were considered of far higher quality and utility by consumers.

The solution personified psychological marketing tactics. It all worked, yielding impressive results.

Score	Good Mistake Rating	Bad Mistake Rating	Ugly Mistake Rating
3			
2			
1			

Lesson(s) Learned: The importance of tailoring your products or services to the needs and desires of the market is critical. It's not what you want to sell, it's what the customers will buy, and what hot buttons can deliver results. This is a simple but often forgotten Marketing 101 rule of thumb.

The client was astute enough to commission market research to investigate a marketplace it wasn't totally familiar with. The results shaped their product offerings into what proved to be a successful launch into a lucrative arena. The "3" rating as a "Good Mistake Rating" is appropriate.

CHAPTER 4

Quantifying Mistakes

"If you can solve a problem, then what is the need of worrying? If you cannot solve it, then what was the use of worrying?"

—Shantdeva

For those interested in quantifying the impact of mistakes and measuring positive or negative results, the use of KPIs (key performance indicators) can enumerate the resulting change.

KPI measure increases or decreases in key business shifts over an evaluated period of time. It can be monthly, quarterly or annual comparisons of hard data. However, the longer the time period between measurements done, the more difficult it will be to react to change. You cannot backtrack change, unfortunately.

Resolving mistakes and issues in hindsight, that is, extended timeframes between carrying out comparatives, is of marginal use, often too late to respond to significant mistakes/changes which become entrenched in your business.

The following Key Performance Indexes (KPI) all provide valid data to measure change, positive or negative, in your business. The objective is to set up an ongoing monitoring schedule to carry out whichever KPI category falls within your concerns.

- Gross sales over a measurable period of time
- Month to month sales
- Sales broken down by product or service
- Unit sales price (increases or decreases)
- Revenue per client
- Discount levels offered
- Regional demographics—origin of sales
- Client retention rate

- Customer attrition numbers
- Current backorders
- Order fulfillment time
- Gross margin overall or by product or service
- Credits, returns, or exceptional post sales discounts issued
- EBITDA (earnings before income tax and depreciation and amortization)
- Results of customer satisfaction surveys
- New customers versus loyal existing clients
- Inventory levels and days/weeks turnover of each item
- Sales calls carried out by your sales force, or qualified new leads secured
- Number of contracts signed, or purchase orders secured
- Visits or clicks on your website, including visits beyond your landing page
- Accounting— changes in supplier payment terms
- Operating expenses analyzed and compared, item by item
- Cash flow days sales outstanding
- Personnel turnover rates, particularly in management
- Employee sick days

Quantifying Missed Opportunities and Statistical Modeling

Missed opportunities are also categorized as mistakes. This can represent anything from a missed sales order to a new product/service launch or marketing campaign. Even an acquisition strategy, for example, which did not realize its goals, or was never initiated, and was a setback for the company.

Every opportunity has a "what if" element. By forecasting what the intended benefits and payback would have represented, net of the costs of implementing that opportunity, and utilizing the appropriate KPI measurement index, the company can estimate the financial cost of its opportunity gain or loss.

Missed opportunities can go beyond financial consequences. For further analysis, there are a number of statistical models that take into account an innumerable series of factors, financial and other benefits, in calculating missed business opportunities. One (of many) such websites is cited in the footnote below.[1]

My company had a very fastidious and renown Parisien pastry chef client whose plans included setting up boutiques in Las Vegas and Toronto.

Our role was to identify and establish a cross-Atlantic liaison for suppliers of highly particular ingredients, including light organic cream (8.6%), buttermilk (4.5%), heavy cream (46%), and Burrata cheese (66%), among numerous others.

Each of his requirements was off-standard and required significant discussions and negotiations with suppliers. Refrigerated samples were continuously shipped over to France for testing and tasting, resulting in another continuous stream of rejections or requests for yet more customization finding their way back to our exhausted team.

Our other roles included competition research, assistance in product pricing, location selection, target customer profiles, and creating a Market Penetration/Launch Strategy.

While this was all fascinating, and often mouth-watering, my nervous client insisted on signing leases for only prime locations in his chosen markets, up to one year before an expected launch date. This, on top of everything else, skewed our data and recommendations.

This represented a significant looming mistake which needed to be dealt with, posthaste, or financial and reputational losses would be incurred by them, and by us.

The mistakes were fixable. We survived and succeeded in expeditiously fulfilling his demands. His requests were not wishes and desires but more like commands, a communications style to which we had to accustomed ourselves.

To this very day I see his products on the shelves of boutique bakeries and confectioners, and I smile, recollecting the sleepless nights, and the

[1]"Opportunity cost in business is the value of the next-best alternative you give up when you make a decision. It's not about the money you spend—it's about the benefits you miss out on." How to Calculate Opportunity Cost (With Examples), https://www.volopay.com/.

trays of 46 percent whipped cream that our project team were obliged to taste test as my client's focus group.

Score	Good Mistake Rating	Bad Mistake Rating	Ugly Mistake Rating
3			
2			
1			

Lesson(s) Learned: Time was not on our side, and neither was the comfort level with the client. My mistake was simply bending to every whim of the demanding and overbearing client in an effort to serve. Sometimes, it just does not work and is not worth the effort. Think carefully about who you are selling to, and under what terms.

"Fixable" was a stretch, and consumed a great deal of our time and effort to accommodate. Ultimately, the deliverables were met. However, this project became the yardstick of the kind of clients/contracts we should ***not*** *take on. A "3" in the "Bad Mistake Rating" was a perfect fit.*

CHAPTER 5

Even the Big Boys Make Mistakes

"Not everything that is faced can be changed. But nothing can be changed until it is faced"

—James Baldwin

There are numerous examples of well-recognized "big boys" who have made substantial business blunders. They are presented here as a learning experience, and in the hope that you might recognize any distress, or a lost or fading opportunity in a shorter timeframe than they did, and feel less "alone."

In an "ostrich with its head in the sand" syndrome, Kodak, the actual inventor of the digital camera, refused to launch into the digital marketplace in an effort to try to protect its firm grip on film technology that the entire marketplace knew was becoming horse and buggy.

Nokia, the early industry leader in cellphones, ignored the emergence of touch screen technology. Their decline was historic. Come to think of it, Blackberry had the same touchscreen blindness and joined Nokia in cellphone obscurity.

When Starbucks first decided to launch into the Chinese market, it made the corporate-blindness, arrogant assumption that the consumer craving for coffee was universal. It was not. There was a necessary learning curve, conducted through awareness-building rather than a Viking-style attack on the marketplace. China's drink of choice had always been tea, and the consumer was not accustomed to paying inflated prices for a new, untested drink. Starbucks marketing prevailed, and a new "cool" generation (teen to young 30s) of dedicated Starbucks coffee fans became the market focus. Error identified, lesson learned. Persistence works.

Coca-Cola launched "New Coke," misjudging consumer interests and tastes, assuming buyers were clamoring for options. New Coke competed with Coke and stole its own market share in this miscue. It only took 79 days to backfire, during which time Pepsi was testing a similar disaster-in-the-making.

There was also the infamous Blockbuster-Netflix scenario where Blockbuster was offered Netflix for a purchase price of 50 million dollars. Blockbuster refused, assuming that the future was in video rentals and pricy downloads instead of streaming. Netflix went on to be worth 150 billion dollars, and Blockbuster moved on to oblivion.

Pets.com decided to take on PetSmart, and open new mega stores next to or close to its well—entrenched competitor. Competing with glitzy, costly marketing and a host of lost leader products was its infamous strategy to capture market share. It misjudged existing customer loyalty and a saturated marketplace as it fizzled into the ether of jumbo failures. Pets.com was eventually bought by PetSmart in December, 2000.

And, of course, the business world will never forget Ford's Edsel, the car of tomorrow which died as a laughingstock, and Enron, the highly unethical and immorally heinous fraud that destroyed untold 401Ks.

Mega-failure examples cannot be concluded without a nod to Japan's SoftBank, and its investment arm, Vision Fund. Trying to reverse its multibillion Yen losses and insurance liabilities, SoftBank allowed its Vision Fund to make a number of questionable (reckless) investments. One such gem was WeWork, an outdated office sharing business model that was quickly becoming obsolete thanks to the technology of mobile offices and communications. WeWork accumulated a $10.7 billion loss by 2023, and even then, attempted a comeback with SoftBank's blessing and yet more funding sacrificed in a losing cause. Why couldn't they have foreseen the depth of WeWork bottomless pit of financial losses? Stop digging when you are digging yourself into a hole.

And here's one closer to home. I was Group Controller for a conglomerate of 26 manufacturing and distribution companies, one of which was a very large forestry and lumber facility. As you can imagine, it produced a huge amount of wood waste and fiber which the operations paid exorbitant fees to haul away and dispose of.

After carrying out market research, I identified a product called "wood flour" which had evident demand, since there were few producers. This was a finely ground fiber (non-nutrative cellulose filler) product used in plastics, pharmaceuticals, and even food additives.

On numerous occasions, I presented this opportunity to upper management, but they were locked into mainstream thinking, and wood flour was anything but. I eventually left the company, secured investment, contracted to haul away raw materials that lumber mills were eager to rid themselves of, at $0 to me, presold 100 percent of the pending production of wood flour into a hungry marketplace, and built and operated a successful venture. Here was a prime example of a company wearing blinders and forgoing a viable opportunity. I was okay with that.

There are more, like Yahoo, Sears, Toys "R" Us, and others undertaking major closures and cutbacks, and only tempting obscurity like CVS, Walgreens, Kroger Groceries, Quicksilver, and Billabong Clothing, all part of an exhaustive lists of big guys misreading markets, stubborn to change, not adopting technology and e-commerce, ignoring evident trends in consumer buying habits, and generally misguidedly hoping and anticipating that their aging business models would prevail.

The lesson to be learned here is simple in nature, but more difficult to implement.

Change is unstoppable, so change or vanish.

A multinational lighting fixture company, one of my clients, had a horrible case of arrogance and complacency that was clashing with a rapidly changing global market environment. It was so ingrained that it was impacting their decision-making abilities.

Asian competitors were outbidding and outpacing them, but they held to their belief that the firms' long-established brand would carry them through. Such was the danger of living in the glorious past when they dominated the market, and downplaying that my client had a clear target on its back that others were zeroing in on, with increasing success.

Their marketplace was becoming cutthroat, and while competitors focused on "good enough" products at discounted pricing and special terms of sale, my behemoth client maintained that their gold standard and name was worth the higher pricing.

Wrong. My role was to engage their old-school management and Board and provide evidence as to how their admirable but outdated modus operandi was leading them into a pending pitfall of marketplace obscurity. This was a market that now cast aside the stodgy supplier hierarchy in favor of lower prices offered by the lowest bidder, regardless of past business dealings.

This was their mistake, and a potentially fatal, ugly one at that.

This was a game my clients were not accustomed to playing.

My strategy was a shakeup of mindset, bottom-line expectations, production cost controls and even several "old guard" managers locked into yesterday's thinking.

The climax of this initiative came when my client lost a $20 million contract with a long-time customer over a pricing difference of $0.05 a lighting fixture. They would not budge, despite the outreach efforts of the buyer who was displaying a modicum of customer loyalty in doing so, to no avail.

My client lost the order and, just as importantly, was in the process of losing an important buyer. For the sake of what? Headstrong and inflexible thinking and an avoidance of recognizing and dealing with their ugly mistake.

I laid out a projected market and competitor analysis demonstrating how they were "dinosaur thinking" themselves into obscurity and potential extinction.

My somewhat jarring and Machiavellian efforts worked. That, and the recently lost huge contract that rattled my client's foundational assumptions combined to force a major corporate rethink.

Within one year, my client had carried out the internal operational, product design and cost control changes recommended, rebranded itself, shed its stodgy image, and repositioned the company as an aggressive industry leader.

Just as importantly, I worked to train their key marketing and sales teams in how to understand and deal with the bullseye target on their back.

Its mistake was its capital for change.

Score	Good Mistake Rating	Bad Mistake Rating	Ugly Mistake Rating
3			
2			
1			

Lesson(s) Learned: There is no place in business for arrogance and complacency. Either can destroy you. Both are personal mindsets that should remain outside your business decision-making environment. They can cloud your judgment and create situations which are serious, but can hopefully be dealt with, sometimes to the business's advantage. In this case, it was a wakeup call that was turned into an advantage. While adapting to shifting markets and hungry competition is often painful, the need to react to change is often "life or death" for a business.

The lighting fixture multinational company scenario is rated as a "good mistake" but earned a rating of "2" on the "Mistakes Outcome and Impact Chart." They reacted slowly and only after there was a decided decline in revenues. It proved to be an important learning curve for them. The recovery was slow, but steady, reflecting a new "outward looking attitude" adopted by their salesforce.

SECTION TWO

Strategic Planning and Setting Core Business Values and Direction

The following chapters are geared toward planning your business, early stage launches, and also for established companies launching new products or services.

Mistakes are both your roadblocks and your opportunities. They are often unavoidable. Mistakes simply happen, but how you recognize, deal with, and learn from business missteps is critical.

Getting it wrong can represent a loss of time, resources, and prospects for future success.

Conversely, getting it right enhances your chances of coming out on top by building a strong foundation.

Nothing guarantees success, but you certainly want to "stack the deck" to assure circumstances play out in your favor.

CHAPTER 6

The Yellow Brick Road to Entrepreneurship

"We cannot solve our problems with the same thinking we used when we created them."

—Albert Einstein

Nature abhors straight lines. They are rarely, if ever, seen on hills, waterways, mountains or trails.

Business pathways likewise meander, ramble, and often encounter crossroads that demand you pivot your direction, sometimes without a clear roadmap of those turnoffs.

But most importantly, the Yellow Brick Road to entrepreneurship, and beyond, is ripe for mistakes. It is part of the learning process that redirects you into being a better businessperson.

Entrepreneurship is a tough road. Every detour, roadblock or hairpin curve offers up challenges. Each can represent a "mistake in the making."

- Impatience, an oft-cited entrepreneurial trait, is a trigger for knee-jerk reactions and errors in judgment. Mistakes ensue.
- Success often breeds complacency which, in turn, ignores or downgrades missteps.
- The longer mistakes are ignored, the steeper the cost and risks involved in finally taking corrective action.
- Make decisions where your actions are timely and definitive. Time is not your friend here.
- Businesspeople who face rejection can often lapse into a "pity me" mindset instead of tackling problems head-on. "Just stay at it" needs to be the rallying cry.

- Take care of yourself. Entrepreneurship is demanding and stressful. The emotionally or physically sapped businessperson makes more errors than their motivated and involved counterparts.

And entrepreneurship demands a balance at work.

- Too many mistakes, and there is likely an issue with your business model and your core mission. You find yourself constantly putting out fires. Business growth becomes secondary, replaced by "survival."
- Not making any (or very few) mistakes? Adversity breeds strength and knowledge. You may be missing out, and when mistakes surface, and they usually do, you might be ill-prepared to deal with them.

The balance is recognizing and dealing with mistakes, miscues, errors, and slipups. **A mistake is a mistake, be it good; to be capitalized on; bad; in need of remedial action; or ugly; putting out the blazing inferno; or walking away.**

Business mistakes demand attention.

Stages in Learning from Mistakes

1. **RECOGNITION**. The first stage, and possibly the most difficult to accept, is that you have erred. Something has gone wrong, but there are no details as of yet as to what that might be, except in general terms. Something is amiss, and you are determined to find out what and why.
2. **ACCEPTANCE**. The process of analysis now begins, with little time wasted on laying blame. That is unconstructive. The important thing is to clearly identify the issues and determining "what's next."
3. **IDENTIFYING CAUSES**. Explore what transpired, and, more importantly, why. This will help shape the priority nature of the mistake and begin to lay the groundwork to ensure that it does not get repeated. Start documenting everything and every step.

4. **EVALUATING ITS IMPACT**. Determination of how serious the situation is by measuring the financial, qualitative, and operational impacts. The more serious the potential impact, the greater the need for attention and correction.
5. **RESOLUTION STRATEGIES**. Deal with the best solutions that also have the least impact on the day-to-day goings on of your business. These are the important considerations of developing workable fix strategies.
6. **APPLYING SAFEGUARDS**. Institute a "checks and balance" system to ensure that mistakes are quickly identified with sufficient lead time for them to be dealt with expeditiously. Preferably the safeguards may raise red flags downstream to help avoid mistakes before they themselves cause distress.
7. **SHARE AND TEACH**. Your team and support staff should all be apprised of the mistakes and concerns and be given an opportunity to offer changes and solutions that may eliminate conditions that have bred the mistake(s) in question. "Fix and do not repeat" are keystones.

I had a large client in the liquid nitrogen business. He had huge freezer units used to treat and keep fruit and vegetables "fresh" so they could be sold off-season at higher margins. The law of supply and demand. Those crisp, fresh apples you buy in the winter, wondering where they mostly come from? Well, now you know.

The client used my company to research the merits and integrity of any new, large-scale company inquiring about using their facilities. I was prescreening for them, running interference with tire kickers so that the liquid nitrogen company's people who were very tech driven, and not terribly market savvy, could focus on what they did best.

Their client base was often unsophisticated and sometimes cash strapped. In the past, my client had been saddled with freezers full of produce that were sliding toward their best before date. Even the magic of liquid nitrogen was time-limited, and expensive.

And then there was Captain Julius.

One referral they unloaded on me was done so with a hearty chuckle on their part. I was curious to meet the prospect. His name was Captain Julius. Not Julius, as he corrected me, but Captain Julius.

Having spent his adulthood in the Congo, while it was still untamed (and before it became "The Democratic Republic of …"), the good Captain Julius (never simply "Julius") was an adventure seeker, having lived in a number of obscure native villages. He professed to have a flair for natural and herbal as well as animal-sourced remedies. As a village doctor/medicine man, he acquired considerable knowledge of these potions mostly unheard of in western medicine. My interest was peaked.

Some were tested by the captain himself, while others were less so. The one he had approached my client with, and was fervent in claiming its miraculous therapeutic properties, was ground lion testicles, particularly those forfeited (most unwillingly) by mature lions roaming "the forest-savanna mosaic habitats, on the Batéké Plateau which spans Gabon, Republic of Congo, and the Democratic Republic of the Congo."

When we met, Captain Julius was serious and promptly covered my desk with bottles containing what I assumed were ground lion testicles swimming lazily in a reddish, yellow solution. I was not tempted. His aim was to freeze-dry and package the milled lion genitalia to be sold as aphrodisiacs.

My first, most obvious question was "How did you get these into the country?" The captain remained stoic, other than exhibiting a brief smirk.

The captain stated he was ready to launch his venture, and, once my nausea passed, I felt very, very compelled to save him from this business disaster in the making.

I offered my counsel, with a straight face; get import permits and licensing to bring in endangered animal "by-products" (although the lions would have likely disputed the term "by-products"); contract laboratory efficacy testing and analysis; do market research to identify market need and acceptance; contact pharmaceutical companies to gauge their interest in refining and marketing; seek out funders willing to invest, and include the creation of a feasibility study and Business Plan.

I graciously offered to do the study and the plan for only $575,000. That was my "go to–go away" technique for nuisance prospects. He heartily agreed, and set off to secure the funding, never to be heard from again.

It was also my way of helping Captain Julius avoid a fatal mistake in probably depleting his life savings to launch this business, which was based on dreadful assumptions too numerous to count.

For Captain Julius, not just "Julius," this incident would serve up a rating of "3" in the Ugly Mistake Rating column of the "Mistakes Outcome and Impact Chart" as per below. Proceeding, under any circumstances, would have been fatal for him (and, undoubtedly, some neutered lions).

Rumor has it that the captain has learned to appreciate the complexities and demands of entrepreneurship, with our help, and, at last count, was considering another less demanding but equally creative initiative. Something to do with training monkeys for repetitive assembly line work. Good luck, Captain.

Score	Good Mistake Rating	Bad Mistake Rating	Ugly Mistake Rating
3			
2			
1			

Lesson(s) Learned: Some business ideas, regardless of the seriousness of the entrepreneur who may champion them, need to be quashed posthaste before the stakeholders involved risk all and lose their investment capital. Left unchecked, the harsh reality and the impact of an ugly mistake are often not recognized in time to avoid problems. Walk away quickly.

There's no way to sugar-coat this opportunity. It was unrealizable and, if even considered, would have represented unfathomable amounts of negative public relations for my client. This was the kind of proposed initiative best considered untouchable. Let the proponent dream on. There may be more fertile ground elsewhere for them. A "3" on the ugly scale is a good fit.

CHAPTER 7

"Gentle Reminder" Mistakes: A Genre unto Itself

"If you don't have a dream, how you gonna have a dream come true?"
—Oscar Hammerstein II

There is a classification of mistakes best referred to as **"Gentle Reminders."** They are not good, bad or ugly, but instead deal with entrepreneurial mindset, attitude, and pivotal thinking.

Some of the following are gleaned from my own entrepreneurial forays, but most are behaviors exhibited by some of my legion of mentees, a truly diverse and creative bunch.

1. Acting quickly on what you know little about is not too smart. You are inviting mistakes.
2. You don't need to be 100 percent ready to launch your idea or venture. Quite often, "good enough" will succeed. Embrace that. **Done trumps perfect.** Besides, we know that perfection is Hollywood personified.
3. Decisions need to have a "go/no go" timeline which is often influenced by your confidence and comfort level, but, more often than not, the market, current client needs, etc. Don't rush your decisions, but don't take forever either. Try setting a response timeline for yourself.
4. The world is often not a terribly smart place. Make allowances for incompetence, and even if you know you are the smartest one out there, recognize and accept your own and others' limitations.

5. Trust yourself. There's no conceivable reason to rewrite your Business Plan seven times when the first or second try reflects your corporate direction and vision. Go with it.
6. When creating a website, business proposal or presentation, nothing will get done until you start. Stop staring at the screen.
7. Who is your ideal client? Age grouping? Demographics? Profession? Everything you do, marketing-wise, product or service-wise need to target who will do business with you.
8. There are always voices in an entrepreneur's head; stop or go, left or right, risk versus carefree abandonment, and questions like, "What happens if I fail"? Silence those voices and go with what instinct/gut feel that got you here.
9. When confronted with rejection, just move on. Assume rejection is part of your business growing pains.
10. Don't overthink, especially in the worry department. Overthinking is like putting speed control on your gas pedal. My mantra has always been "I have had many problems in my life, and most of them have never happened."
11. In choosing a mentor, don't select one who agrees with you too much. Your "devil's advocate" mentor is your best friend.
12. Too many entrepreneurs feel that market research is for sissies. Be a market research sissy.
13. View tasks as baby steps. Undertaking too many simultaneously will trip you up and many of your tasks may not be completed properly, or in the right sequence.
14. Never stifle your instincts. You don't need to pursue everything that crosses your creative mind, but don't quickly dismiss them. File stuff for later.
15. Every once in a while, abandon the detail work and step back to take a 20,000 ft. view. Alternate perspectives are your friend.
16. Given a choice between doodling creatively with a scratchpad or grunting away filling in forms or inputting data, the advice is to ditch, delay or delegate everything except the doodling. Your business will thank you for your higher-level mental space contributions.

17. Constantly reinforce your visionary goals and purpose and learn to focus. This will help keep you on track and avoid meandering that can morph into mistakes or lost opportunities.
18. Set your goals slightly higher than readily achievable. Entrepreneurship should be a little painful so that success is better appreciated and more meaningful. Surprise yourself.
19. Recognize risk, but do not embrace it. It's your business aspirations and the opportunities at hand that deserve to be embraced.
20. Simplify your life so that you can focus on your business and thereby avoid mistakes. That implies getting rid of distractions other than anything or anybody who nourishes your entrepreneurial drive.
21. Don't believe just the market research that tells you what you want to hear at the expense of timely input that could be a forebearer of warnings or, better yet, alternate opportunities.
22. Above all, enjoy the entrepreneurial experience. Relish it. Anything less is an open invitation to become complacent or detached. Both of the latter represent business-terminal thinking.

My firm's young technology company client was a wizard in the world of handheld video games. He had several games ranked within the twenty top global packages, and was in the process of creating, what he called, a "disrupter video adventure."

He was articulate, focused, and seemingly unstoppable. Devoting all his resources to this one initiative, the company's staff had quadrupled, and his cash flow paid the price.

The team grew to be unmanageable, especially for the founder, and mid-level managers were hired to manage the masses of programmers and graphic designers. This was followed in rapid succession by a VP Technology, a VP Graphics Creation, and a VP Administration, all of whom brought their ideas and recommendations on board, often at odds with other members of the team, and even the founder.

In an attempt to reign in the firestorm, the founder brought in an Executive VP to oversee the slew of managers and their respective teams.

This effectively isolated the founder from his people, and his company. Decision making, in virtually all key areas of the business, was now delegated to his new army of bright young managers whom, the founder had hoped, would emulate his style and creativity.

This assumption was wishful thinking and a misplacement of authority and reliance. The company had almost reached a point of inertia as some managers strove for position and greater authority. The business was not producing video games as quickly as it was generating a division of responsibilities that was stumbling all over itself and frustrating the founder.

My firm was mandated to review, analyze, assess, and act upon a plan to streamline, create a more end product-oriented focus in a more structured working environment. As well, our goal was to eliminate the roadblocks (i.e., people, politics, positions) that were deemed obstructionist. And we needed to act quickly before the business and the frustrated founder self-destructed.

We defined a prime criterion for everyone, that being "how are you, and your efforts, contributing quantifiable value to the company and to the creation and launch of the 'disrupter video adventure' that was of paramount importance to the future market positioning of the company?"

The results were formidable. A number of managers and the subordinates they hired could not justify their existence within the scope of the prime criterion and were dismissed. Interestingly, the management voids created were not as damaging as was feared. In fact, most were filled by lower rank team members who grew up with the company and shared the founders' dream.

Score	Good Mistake Rating	Bad Mistake Rating	Ugly Mistake Rating
3			
2			
1			

Lesson(s) Learned: While the message here would be "bigger is not better," the main takeaway is that it is critical to stay fiercely engaged to your entrepreneurial dream. Whatever brought you to whatever success you have achieved, let that guide you in future-forward thinking. People's survival skills are often sidelined by their insecurities, as was evident in the storyline just discussed. Don't lose control of who you are and where you want to go.

Sometimes the best of intentions can get away from you as it did with the company's founder. In this case, our suggesting a solution from within the company's ranks delivered the desired results, namely, a team of in-house managers who cared. They were family. The mistake was identified, corrected and provided a valuable learning experience for the founder. A "2" score as a "Good Mistake Rating" is appropriate.

CHAPTER 8

Business Common Sense Is Often Not So Common

"It isn't that they cannot find the solution. It is that they cannot see the problem."

—G. K. Chesterton

Here are a number of what would be categorized as common sense mistakes and unintentional (or possibly intentional) examples of poor business-behavior that can, and likely would cost you.

1. Own your mistakes. Blaming others, especially when those blamed and everyone around them knows it's you. None of this "who me?" please. Owning your mistakes will encourage you to fix them and learn not to repeat the blunders.
2. When launching a business, or in its early blooming phase, the entrepreneur may choose to sell to anyone, regardless of their creditworthiness, and at lost leader prices designed to sway buyers. A cardinal rule: "Don't sell to crooks." Some things never change.
3. Your time is precious. Don't network with people unless you can see what's in it for you to do so.
4. Don't get involved in deals that are too complex, require a small army to come to the table to play, or where the deal is contingent on an "iffy" participant. This type of scenario, while it may be attractive, probably has a small chance of success, and a huge chance of you getting into trouble. Mistakes abound in these complex and convoluted relationships where self-interest prevails.
5. Spend your cash where it does the most good. Yes, when it adds value or opportunities to the business. No, for shiny toys and ego puffballs.

6. A contract, purchase order, memorandum of understanding, strategic partnership agreement; in fact, any purportedly binding document always has an escape door, sometimes blatant and other times camouflaged in legalese. The greatest security is confidence in the signatories. Anything less can be a mistake that might be painful and from which it could be painful to extricate yourself.
7. People are highly protective of their turf, so much so that "Everybody lies…every day, every hour, awake, asleep." (Mark Twain). Knowing and believing that will protect you from making mistakes by trusting those whom you know could and most likely would deceive for their personal gain. That's called blinding greed. Consider this "mistake avoidance" advice.
8. I have repeatedly, ad nauseam, preached that "your first priority, and the focus of everyone working for you, is to create value for your business." Anything else is either overhead or fluff. Ignoring that idiom is sure to cost you. That's how mistakes sneak up on you when you are otherwise engaged.
9. Market research is not just a "make work" task dreamed up by market researchers. It is profoundly important and can keep you and your business on track. Ignoring market research, or only believing just what you want to believe, is a ticket to the mistakes snake pit. This cardinal rule is worth repeating, and I do so throughout this book.
10. If you are undergoing a cash crunch and cutting expenses, don't cut your marketing. That is a huge mistake. In fact, increase outreach costs and campaigns. It is the results of your marketing that can throw you a lifeline.
11. Finally, if your business is experiencing mistakes and blunders, look to yourself first before you cast aspersions onto others around you. Your business mistakes may be home grown.

This happens to be one of my very favorite business stories, and one I was directly involved in, mostly in the capacity of a train-wreck observer.[2]

[2]It has been reprinted here from Jay J. Silverberg, *The Thirty Step Start-up Playbook* (Business Expert Press, 2023).

It is classified as an uncharacteristically stupid mistake, or, as truth would have it, a series of amazingly laughable mistakes.

"There is joy in just the act of planning to launch a business. Part of that is a process of enduring a 'proof of concept' where the idea is floated through various 'prove it to me' stages, impartial research, trusted sounding board input and critical-path planning, all of which precede your 'go/no go' decision.

It's a thought-provoking safety net process, except if you happen to be sophomoric half-wits, or someone so blinded by your own perceived brilliance that you ignore every red flag waving madly in your face.

Meet the Ski Bike inventors and entrepreneurs: two of the Three Stooges whose concept of a bike on skis racing down a ski hill, followed a breakneck path of 'never ever do this in business.'

The third Stooge, incidentally, was in traction for months following a disastrous prototype ski bike test run. He was like the kid Mikey from the Quaker Oats Life Cereal 'Let Mikey try it' commercial. He was the punchline.

He bowed out of the venture. Being accosted and threatened with divorce by his wife was an added incentive, as was the loss of his savings earned selling psychoactive drugs. So, the original idea of a Ski Bike venture was not far removed from his likely drug-altered sense of safety.

But none of this deterred the two remaining partners from shushing full speed down the slopes of mishap and business failure. They were legends in their own cluttered minds. Their story is worth sharing. It exemplifies everything not to do in business and should come with a disclaimer, 'Don't ever try this.'

The two lingering founders called upon me to help them find investors. I declined, but their story was like an accident in the making. I could not look away, so I watched their disaster unfold as a captivated spectator.

Apparently, the Ski Bike was invented during a drunken weekend up at the ski lodge. It was a simple contraption: skis mounted front and back over the wheels and gripping plates installed as brakes to dig into the snow. Ice on the slopes diminished the braking capabilities, but this notion was beyond their ability to focus down on the small but critical details.

The one factor they forgot to entertain was that you really needed to be drunk or pharma-spaced to operate the Ski Bike because, when you fell, or were thrown off, which was a very likely scenario, and a limber body bounced better.

They built a better prototype, 'Ski Bike 2,' which barely lessened the danger but promised greater thrills.

They secured a patent, thinking there would be hordes of potential design infringements when reality proved the exact opposite. They had one hundred percent of the market, whatever that was.

They produced a promotional video, carefully editing out the troubling falls and screams of panic of the on-screen riders. Elastic ethics, right?

They then succeeded in finding an investor, the owner of an idle bicycle factory in China capable of producing the Ski Bikes.

The first batch of Ski Bikes were set up as rentals at a local ski resort. While the founders were astute enough to have riders sign waivers, there was no waiver strong enough to protect them from reckless negligence.

The very first launch at the resort saw the busiest several days for the Ski Patrol, as most Ski Bike users were rescued and carted away in various states of personal disrepair.

It was all downhill from here.

Before 'Ski Bikes 2' could be redesigned and introduced, the lawsuits threatening the business mounted. The Chinese investor turned off the cash-flow taps and the business collapsed, just like their Ski Bikes.

No market research, no real product testing, no product safety engineering, no feasibility, no risk analysis, no budgeting: a business idea built on naivete, brashness, and endorphins.

Several months ago, I actually saw an ad selling a used Ski Bike. 'Used only once' it said, and that spoke volumes."

Its rating outcome and impact that follow were well deserved.

Score	Good Mistake Rating	Bad Mistake Rating	Ugly Mistake Rating
3			
2			
1			

Lesson(s) Learned: When mistakes materialize, followed by another, and yet another, the prudent action is to run, don't just walk away. If you are digging yourself into a hole, stop digging. In the case of Ski

Bikes, serious errors in judgment created a tidal wave of dangerous mistakes that materialized in such rapid succession that fixing any aspect of the business was impossible. These "entrepreneurs" were too married to their idea, and the spontaneity of business model flaws, what one would regard as dangerously uncommon thinking, were the order of the day. Ski bikes are an extreme example and an epitome of ludicrous, rapid-fire mistakes and are now a regular example of what NOT to do, in my lecture series.

Ugly idea, confluence of ugly decisions and a nasty outcome. This case epitomizes a "3" on the "Ugly Mistake Rating," only because there is no 4 or 5 on the scale to better exemplify the absurdity and danger of the Ski Bike fiasco.

CHAPTER 9

Mistakes Are Your Capital and Creating Opportunities

"Every problem is a gift. Without them we wouldn't grow."

—Tony Robins

Steve Jobs epitomizes "mistakes create opportunities." Others' mistakes, not his. In 1976 Jobs cofounded Apple and helped develop the Macintosh computer. In 1985, amid internal jockeying and power struggles, Jobs quit Apple. Between 1985 and 1997, Jobs acquired the graphics arm of Lucasfilm and created Pixar, the creator of Toy Story and other animated mega-successes. At Pixar's prime, Jobs sold the company to Disney Studios in 1986 for $4.7 billion. In 1997, Apple, on the verge of bankruptcy, persuaded Jobs to return as CEO. Steve Jobs accumulated 960 international patents including 323 Apple patents. The company he spearheaded had a 2025 market value of $4.8 trillion, the third most valuable company in the world.

When anyone mentions "mistakes create opportunities," Steve Jobs' name always leaps into the forefront.

Of course, entrepreneurs are not all Steve Jobs. But, nevertheless, there are numerous strategies to avoid mistakes, or to transform blunders into winning possibilities.

Mistakes Happen

Nobody has a monopoly on business missteps, gaffes, and blunders.

Business can also be unforgiving and is an impatient taskmaster.

Own your mistakes, analyze what went wrong, extract invaluable lessons, add that newfound knowledge to your ability to cope and build on, and thereby adding skills of better decision making in the future.

It often requires commitment to **honest personal reflection**, revisiting the business skills you have honed, and the **self-actualization** of your "talents and potentialities": lessons that can augment your business knowledge and further enhance your entrepreneurial capabilities.

Get on with it.

A Shopping List of Crucial Questions to Ask Yourself

WHAT WENT WRONG? Have you identified the issues and challenges at hand? This seems like an obvious starting point, but mistakes often get masked with other simultaneous events, and it is necessary to isolate the concerns themselves in order to deal with them effectively. Anything less is simply dancing around the missteps.

HOW SERIOUS IS IT? Fully understanding the implications of the threat and the short, medium, and long-range impacts it will have on your business is a crucial component of the problem-solving process. This will also help you prioritize the action planning you intend to undertake and how quickly you may need to act.

WHAT WAS THE CAUSE? How did it come about? Knowing the source is not intended as laying blame, but more so understanding how it all transpired, what gaps became chasms, how your people reacted, and what the causes were. This becomes the baseline for action.

WHAT IS THE QUANTIFIABLE IMPACT? Every mistake has quantifiable results. These can be financial, market share, or directly linked to lost opportunities such as contracts and proposals. The ability to measure these impacts is part of the learning curve to understand and react to business errors.

WHAT IS THE QUALITATIVE IMPACT? Business missteps may have a qualitative impact such as damage to your reputation in the marketplace. This represents an opportunity for you to enhance and rebuild your market presence while repairing damage that may have been done.

WAS IT EXPECTED OR ANTICIPATED? Making mistakes is inevitable. They are either the result of a slowly brewing situation or conflict within your company, or a "jack-in-the-box" surprise thrust upon you. Identifying how the mistake evolved and presented itself helps you handle it and assures that the source is effectively dealt with.

HAVE YOU FULLY EMBRACED THE EVENT? You are the business and all those around you reflect your skills and expectations. When mistakes occur, you are ultimately responsible. Delegating blame to others is not productive, nor does it represent a solution.

WHAT IS THE CORRECTIVE ACTION NECESSARY, IF ANY? Developing a plan of action to implement correction action is critical. Delivering on the plan is equally important. These are part of business survival skills that will serve you well and represent an opportunity to grow.

WHAT HAVE YOU LEARNED? Your ability to accept what consequences mistakes have dealt you and your effort to react in an effective and expeditious manner are part of the learning process. Embrace a learning mindset. You can even learn from others. Role modeling is an effective strategy to employ. Moving forward is a key benefit of learning from others how to cope with mistakes. These represent an opportunity for you to become a better-equipped leader. Mistakes inspire creative problem solving as part of your toolbox.

DID YOU SHARE THE NEWFOUND KNOWLEDGE WITH YOUR PEOPLE? Mistakes generate newfound knowledge, enhanced business skills, and the opportunity to recognize the need to change. This newfound knowledge should be shared with your people so that your team acts in a cohesive manner. Hence the meaning of "team."

IS THE SOLUTION NOW PART OF YOUR CORPORATE THINKING? Mistakes teach you and others around you by way of demanding solutions that are timely and effective. This can create a learning culture where everyone impacted is sensitized to the need of constantly being on guard for pending or brewing concerns and acting in the best interest of the company.

CAN IT HAPPEN AGAIN? A mistake highlights gaps in your operation, or style of management/entrepreneurial thinking. Make sure you understand, recognize, and plug that gap.

ARE THERE IDENTIFIED OPPORTUNITIES THAT YOU CAN TAKE AWAY FROM THIS? Mistakes can often be equal parts recognition, distress, acceptance, resolution, and opportunity. The latter is an important component and should always be integral in the solution process.

CAN THIS CONTRIBUTE TO THE GROWTH OF YOUR BUSINESS? Adapting to change, or the ability to recognize that mistakes can bring about positive change is an important milestone in the process. Make sure, in moving forward, you remain alert to "mistakes in progress," that is, identifying issues as they may be arising, and not just putting out fires once they have landed in your lap.

HAS THIS CHANGED YOUR MINDSET AND FUTURE BEHAVIOR? The answer had better be yes. Whatever goes wrong should ultimately transform these events into success and growth, both professionally and personally, rather than moments of embarrassment.

ARE YOU NOW A SMARTER AND BETTER DECISION MAKER? Innovation, creativity, adaptability, and the willingness to change are cornerstone skills that the process delivers. Accepting these essential qualities will greatly enhance your decision-making abilities. Further, you will inspire those around you to hone their problem-solving talent.

WILL THIS EVENT MAKE YOU A STRONGER BUSINESSPERSON, MORE READY FOR THE NEXT ENGAGEMENT? Overcoming any fear of failure will help you face future incidents, and there's no greater teacher than successfully instilling survival and coping skills that become part of your business instincts.

DID YOU TAKE THIS GAFFE PERSONALLY? Business is not and should not be personal. You can keep repeating this mantra. Failing to separate the two worlds you inhabit will likely lead to errors in judgment where solutions will be crafted more so to protect yourself personally rather than to bring about positive outcomes for the business.

Rethink How to Capitalize on Mistakes

- An inflexible mindset stifles learning possibilities. Opportunities abhor rigid thinking.
- Be a risk-taker to whatever degree you are comfortable, and then add bit more.
- Think about growth and opportunities. Do not limit yourself to the easy and obvious. That's a mistake that will cost you.
- When you mess up, and we all do, let blunders open up new options to do better. Opportunities can capitalize on thinking beyond the staid and everyday blinders that we all wear.

- Consider a mistake as step one in identifying and trying alternative strategies and scenarios.
- Simply fixing a mistake is a band-aid solution. Dig deeper. Fix the mistakes' source or gap that allowed the blunder to surface.
- Own your mistakes. Guilt does dissipate and makes you more amenable to accept change.
- Foster innovation in everything you do, every plan you make.
- Don't focus on allocating blame. It's dead-end thinking.
- Surround yourself with freethinkers, not those who agree with everything you say and do. Communication is your lifeline to turning mistakes into more worthwhile end-results. Problem solving is best achieved as a team sport.
- Practice "acceptable risk." Anything beyond acceptable will test your ability to adopt corrective action that might invite productive change.
- You cannot act until you understand what went wrong and why. That becomes a springboard for next-level planning that can encompass new thinking and new probabilities and prospects.
- Most things are fixable. Look on failure and blunders as challenges.
- Opportunities show up at the strangest times and materialize from the oddest, often most unexpected sources. Even serious gaffs have opportunity portals. Stay alert.
- Trust your instincts. This bears repeating. If your instincts are to do nothing, or panic or fret, or mutter your self-protective mantra, "Why Me?" you will be oblivious to opportunities. Change your focus. Or go get a job.
- It's always good to think "newly improved," but the old ways worked for a reason. Don't simply abandon them. Build on them.
- Converting mistakes to opportunities is best accomplished with baby steps. Jumping headfirst into new territory is foolish and ill-advised. Balance on the precipice of change before leaping in.
- Finally, recognize that missteps are an integral part of entrepreneurship. The sooner you embrace that fact, the quicker you will open yourself up to the opportunities that are often embedded in mistakes.

A "Good Mistake Rating" Business Story

Mux (pseudonym) presented an interesting case. The company had invented a cabling connector that eliminated the need for miles of costly coaxial cable in high rise complexes. Within six months, Mux had accumulated almost two years of backorders at their current rate of production.

Component supply chains were straining to try to keep up. Production was increased, but not nearly enough to meet demand. Mux did not dare go offshore since their intellectual property (IP) was their main capital. Interesting problems at the deeper end of the pool. But, nonetheless, serious.

On its own, Mux had taken a number of steps, mostly in panic mode, which foretold imminent disaster.

My company and I were called in to help solidify its position and future growth that was being so evidently exhibited.

We created a Business Plan that exuded Mux's success as well as adopting a realize growth strategy. The forecasts were supported by purchase orders and letters of commitment from major clients. Production throughput was cast in an augmented, modular schedule that could be met with the right conditions and "just in time" inventory control.

Next, there was an urgent need for funding. The cash requirements to feed its inventory needs and finance its accounts receivable and production had Mux in a chokehold. Banks, being conservative in nature, were highly suspicious of this phenomenal growth of the business. Those who did not reject Mux outright, mostly before we were brought on board, offered terms and constraints that did little to alleviate the skyrocketing growth that Mux was undergoing.

We reached out to investors and venture capital players who could not only provide funding but could also help stabilize Mux's management team. Investors who could provide funding alone without delivering additional value for the business were cast aside.

To protect the IP, we assumed copyrights and patents were insufficient. We worked with an aeronautical epoxy supplier to find a way to embed the key chips into an impenetrable molded casing. It worked.

Sales were not a problem, but production was. We moved Mux to a larger and high security facility and had all Mux's staff and managers, and suppliers, sign a Letter of Confidentiality and an NDA.

The last area of concern was "What's next?" We encouraged Mux to establish a product development lab. Mux's success was already giving birth to competitors, and it was of utmost importance, we felt, for Mux to stay a few steps ahead, which they did.

Having covered all the bases, we proudly watched Mux fulfill its potential. From a somewhat accidental/"fluke" invention and a house full of growing pain problems to a thriving enterprise that eventually went public on the stock exchange.

Score	Good Mistake Rating	Bad Mistake Rating	Ugly Mistake Rating
3			
2			
1			

Lesson(s) Learned: Identify the challenges in your business, both those that can generate a negative or positive impact, prioritize them in terms of which have the greatest potential consequence, and tackle them accordingly. Move forward and adapt, adapt, adapt. Too many businesspeople have pressing issues that they simply don't want to or fear dealing with. The longer that an issue goes untreated, the more likely it will move up the destruction hierarchy. Your business will suffer.

Great business, but it needed to reboot their operation to keep up with the market demand and to protect their technology, all of which they acknowledged were in danger. Following their uptake of our recommendations, they prospered instead of just putting out fires created by rampant growth, earning themselves a "3" as poster-worthy on the "Good Mistake Rating" scale.

An "Ugly Mistake Rating" Business Story

I was introduced to Michael at an investment conference. The fact that it was a junior mining conference should have been my first clue. He was presented as a highly successful and trustworthy money manager with few credentials forthcoming which should have been my second red flag.

I knew full well that the terms "successful money manager" and "junior mining" were most often not synonymous with each other, but I soldiered on.

Michael was the kind of in-your-face promoter that nature abhors, but, somewhere in your mind, there is a meandering thought that he could make you a lot of money. I now believe that is called "discomforting greed."

Early on in our relationship Michael proposed an investment scenario via a Public Market Reverse Takeover or a Pink Sheet launch, both, as I learned, were the core vehicles for the get-rich-quick artists. Michael proved himself to be such an artist, somewhat stumbling and inept, but definitely a player among fellow greasy performers. But I did not latch onto this until much later. Greed, apparently, is a great camouflaging agent.

Michael's attraction to me was that I had a going concern, and a genuine above-board company with a strong market presence, far different than the bikini car wash franchise he had just finished promoting. Again, a credibility clue I failed to recognize as a danger sign.

Documents were drawn up, and a share distribution was agreed to. This type of transaction demands a host of regulatory documentation, and all required my signature. When none appeared, Michael simply waved it off, stating that it was all taken care of. My Spidey senses were now tingling.

I demanded to review everything that was to be submitted to market regulators and, upon a cursory review, there were two things that were evident: (1) Michael's name did not appear anywhere, not as Director or Officer. When I inquired about this, Michael shrugged it away by saying that he was always the person behind-the-scenes in these transactions. My suspicions grew exponentially, and (2) my own signature appeared throughout the paperwork to be filed, but I had never signed anything. On closer examination, I noticed that every one of my signatures was identical. Obviously cut and pasted.

I was done. I informed Michael that I was not going anywhere near this deal and would be informing the regulatory powers that I was terminating the application process.

The furor that ensued with a bitter Michael was straight out of a low-budget Hollywood bad guy-good guy movie. It was both concerning and entertaining, and over quickly. Michael had other projects to pump (and pimp).

Score	Good Mistake Rating	Bad Mistake Rating	Ugly Mistake Rating
3			
2			
1			

Lesson(s) Learned: Certainly, your mother likely tried to drill this home to you: Don't deal with people who try too hard to befriend you. Embrace your instincts above all else and stay away from the dark side. Simple enough lessons that even Yoda (i.e., Star Wars fame) could have taught you.

If you need an example of a "3" rating on the ugly mistake scale, this is it. Succumbing to greed and wearing rose-colored glasses are not just cliches. They can blind you. Beware.

CHAPTER 10

Embracing Mistakes and Getting Past Them

"I have not failed. I've just found 10,000 ways that won't work"
—Thomas Edison (On finally inventing the lightbulb)

From early childhood right through to adulthood we learn to deflect blame. As we grow, mistakes are perceived as failures and signs of weakness. In all cases, regardless of age, we are conditioned that mistakes and punishment go together. Mistakes have consequences.

Learning to embrace mistakes in businesses demands going against our instincts and everything we have learned. Nonetheless, embracing mistakes is a vital exercise that can provide huge payback and opportunity for your business.

There is a plethora of mistakes that businesspeople fall into which stem from either personal and/or professional traits, any of which would impact their business.

Personal Traits That Can Lead to Mistakes	Professional Traits That Can Lead to Mistakes
Misgivings and insecurity	Error in judgment
Family/personal pressures	Buyers' remorse
Uncertainty, difficulty deciding	Being overwhelmed with work
Intolerance of self	Decision-making difficulties
Nagging feelings of pending doom	Second-guessing yourself
Hoping for the best	Mistakes with a client
Refusing to accept blame	Mistakes relating to a product or service
Allowing doubt or fear to govern your actions	Customer service shortcomings

These represent a small handful of situations that might lead you to deflect mistakes and avoid embracing and dealing with blunders.

- First and foremost, understand that business mistakes do not define you. Dealing with mistakes is stressful enough without beating yourself up. Treat yourself with kindness.
- It takes a conscious and concerted effort for the businessperson to change their thinking and learn to embrace mistakes, both theirs and others, and foster a safe culture and environment for themselves and the employees to deliver growth and opportunities.
- Admit errors. Transparency, including proposed solutions, is likely to be well received by your team, customers, and suppliers alike. Taken one step further, that being public apologies, where deemed necessary, turn mistakes into market strengths. Empathy reigns, since nobody out there is mistake-free.
- A byproduct of embracing mistakes and encouraging your team to do likewise creates a safety net wherein change or innovation is encouraged without excessive judgment.
- Embracing mistakes does not imply also targeting perfection. In resolving issues, "better, but not always best" is generally acceptable.
- Mistakes provide fodder for future growth. This applies to products or services, technology, marketing, branding, opportunity implementation considerations, and essential planning. The term is "**smart mistakes**," that is, business errors that deliver valuable insight that drives benefits for the company.
- Once a mistake is embraced and effectively dealt with, conducting a thorough debriefing and after-action review is highly recommended. Insights as to cause and source of mistakes is yet another important component of dealing head-on with business missteps.
- The faster you embrace mistakes the faster you can expedite a solution. Tackling blunders without delay is a wise practice.
- Learning from and acting upon your slip up is more effective than simply trying to predict its lingering consequences.
- Since working for yourself can be an exciting venture, the advent of gaffes can be trying. All the more reasons to recognize, resolve, and move past them.
- One other suggestion might be to document what transpired so that you can refer to past incidents when similar errors reoccur.

- Accepting mistakes quickly and with integrity can build credit with those impacted by the blunder. This is an opportunity to build your image and credibility and sets a positive example for those associated with you.

Slips happen. They cannot be ignored and should not be sloughed off to others. They are yours to own and wear. Embracing mistakes is not only a critical component of running a business, but they can also be invaluable "stepping stones" to growth, and change.

Getting past mistakes can be the key to sustainable business evolution devoid of nagging unresolved problems that would otherwise surely stalk you.

Our client was a high-end women's design house whose reputation was built on bringing exclusive fashions to a boutique marketplace. They were successful for many years until overseas "knock-off" producers decided that my client was fair game.

Try as they might, within several days after launching their latest fashion lines, copies would hit the market at a fraction of my client's pricing. They literally had two to three days to own the market before their dealers were flooded with inexpensive copycats.

This trend was potentially disastrous for my client. Its style and designs were its IP which was being breached with impunity and great regularity.

My company was called in to help. As objective observers, we were mandated to identify the issues, sources, and conflicts, and provide workable recommendations, all of which we did.

The company's mistake was being lax about their IP. While they implemented certain secrecy protocols, they were insufficient to thwart the outflow of trade secrets.

Identifying the sources and leakage was easy enough, and remedies were harsh and swift. But that was the simple part. Stemming future sabotage was the true mandate.

First, during the actual fashion design phase, we seconded the design staff in comfortable but secure surroundings. They were left to complete their tasks in a controlled environment. Each of them had previously passed a test of confidentiality and nondisclosure.

Once the designs were completed, production was distributed among several facilities, each generating components, but none with any knowledge of the end products.

One secure assembly facility was created for final assembly, and once the designs were consumer-ready, they were shipped out by armored trucks directly to the key retailers. Imagine that.

"First to market" was an aggressive launch strategy that set the tone for my client as the market leader in their sector and sent the copycat producers into a catch-up frenzy that gave my client sufficient time to own their market niche.

Finally, since word had spread about the breach perpetrated upon my client, we helped design a public apology to persuade its loyal following to return to the fold. They did.

This combination of remedial activity worked extremely well. Leakage was eliminated. IP was now well-protected, sales flourished, and my clients' brand was stronger than ever.

Score	Good Mistake Rating	Bad Mistake Rating	Ugly Mistake Rating
3			
2			
1			

Lesson(s) Learned: Identifying and admitting to mistakes is often easier than dealing with them and moving forward stronger than ever. Remedial action may demand taking initiatives on a number of fronts. An effective businessperson must learn to embrace mistakes, both their own and others on their team, and deal with them all in a manner that is swift and often ruthless, and assuring that it cannot and should not happen again. This course of action often opens up other qualitative and quantitative opportunities for the enterprise, including enhanced market and brand awareness, as was the case with our fashion house client. That becomes a win-win.

Serious challenges cannot be ignored. They don't generally go away by themselves. They demand dramatic action, which is what this company undertook long after the consequences were felt. There was too much of an unnecessary delay in responding. This lag was a bad decision on their part. Threats were unexpectedly severe and relentless, and a major game plan change alleviated risks. The danger was lessened, but a "3" on the "Bad Mistake Rating" was warranted because of their response time.

CHAPTER 11

Are Missed Opportunities Mistakes? Ask Schrodinger's Cat

"Opportunities are like sunrises. If you wait too long, you miss them."
—William Arthur Ward

Missed blunders are often an illusion.

We play mind games; stop or go, now or later, insecurity, indecision, second-guessing, lost moments in time that leave us wondering 'what if'? and, just like that, a mistake has taken hold, and, quite possibly, an opportunity has been wasted. Lost in the foray of "maybes."

Missed opportunities are mistakes, or are they? According to **Schrodinger's Cat**, we may never really know.[3] If missed opportunities remain unknown, they could represent lost and bypassed mistakes that could have dealt a blow to the business but did not because they were not realized, or they could have been positive lapses that could have delivered strong financial results and greater market share but did not because the cat remained locked in the unopened box.

---

[3]"If you've heard of the famous Schrodinger's cat experiment, you'll have a pretty good idea of what it's like to 'regret' an opportunity not taken. Briefly, this is a thought experiment in quantum physics where a cat is hypothetically placed in a box with some harmful substance that can "go off" inside the box at any moment. But since the box is sealed, there is no way to know the cat's fate at any given moment. The catch is that against all common sense, to the quantum physicist, the cat isn't either alive or dead. It's both alive and dead at any point in time. The destiny of any opportunity is forever concealed from us for the simple reason that the key to the box is forever lost."—https://angela-yurchenko.medium.com/why-missed-opportunities-are-the-schrodingers-cat-of-life-6ef8317bcdbe.

Lost opportunities emanating from mistakes are commonplace in business, but, quite often, we do not know what the outcome would have been. If an opportunity seemed good, but was not acted on, reflection tells us it would probably have been very good, and we must have made a big mistake. If the opportunity was questionable or iffy, we are proud and glad not to have stepped into the trap of disaster, but we really don't know. We imagine it all. You have no way of knowing if any of these events played out in your mind are true. Schrodinger's Cat was playing with us.

How do you move on?

1. Analyze and reflect on what transpired, what instigated the mistake? Was it something you did or did not do? Was there a fear factor, or a deep-seated apprehension, and, if so, why? Was it a timing issue, or were circumstances simply not quite right?
2. You can speculate on the missed outcome, but that is simply frustrating and pointless. Instead, identify what caused you to miss out. Not why was it a mistake, but what caused the holdback to act. It could represent a gap or weakness in your decision making which, if so, demands some corrective action, possibly confidence building that creates in you the ability to act, not vacillate.
3. Learn to focus on the opportunities at hand instead of always searching out the shiny coin on the road. Perhaps multitasking is not your strong suit.
4. Regrets abound when mistakes cost you opportunities. They are destructive and harmful to your well-being. Instead, try to look on them as learning experiences so that, next time, action will replace inaction.
5. A missed opportunity can be classified as a mistake when its origin, or cause, is attributable to a lack of (or poor) research, inadequate due diligence that does not draw a conclusion, timing, such as waiting for the ideal timeframe which may be elusive, fear, or an inflexible business operating model that has a narrow field of vision and an inhibition to take risks. These represent but a few **mistake instigators** that sometimes impair even the best entrepreneurs to act decisively.

6. Distinguish between failing to act because of insufficient information or lackluster motivation, or a misunderstanding, versus failure to act because of a priority focus on other matters. A mistake is a mistake. Learn to multitask, or delegate.
7. Missed opportunities, for whatever reasons are sometimes retrievable. More often than not, the entrepreneur will move onto the next one, but some stubborn businesspeople will pursue lost opportunities in an effort to be given another chance. Which is your style?

The key is to stop procrastinating and simply "start doing." The timing will never be perfect, and the outcome may not be as good as you hoped, or as bad as you feared. But, until you open the box, the fear of failure or the ecstasy of pending success remains unknown.

And Schrodinger's Cat will be locked inside.

A business associate had an opportunity to invest in a trivia game that eventually became an international sensation. But of course, when he had the opportunity to invest, it was just an idea at that point.

The time-sensitive investment needed to be in place within two days.

His life at that time was overshadowed by various situations; a pending, very bitter divorce, a major overseas government contract, and a shortage of funds he was not willing to risk.

Being a close friend of the trivia game founders, he agreed to participate. On his way to catch his flight with a highly placed government minister, he wrote a check and left it at his office for his friends to pick up. The amount was $3,000 for which he was entitled to 25 percent of the venture.

In the throes of his divorce, his wife emptied their joint bank account and the $3,000 check bounced. The game founders contacted him several times overseas, but he could not focus on this opportunity he might be forfeiting. He was otherwise occupied.

The game company launched without him. His $3,000 investment would have been worth $11 million within six to eight months.

His mistake was making an investment and commitment without following through and focusing on too many other concurrent issues and events in his professional and personal lives. Obviously, he was not an adept multitasker.

Making quasi-decisions is dangerous without the benefit of tracking inevitably leads to mistakes which, in his case, missing out on an $11 million windfall.

Score	Good Mistake Rating	Bad Mistake Rating	Ugly Mistake Rating
3			
2			
1			

Lesson(s) Learned: The lost opportunity, in this case, was directly attributable to the investor's tenuous situation. He could have made more definitive investment arrangements and taken greater interest in his opportunity. He did no research and simply threw $3,000 to placate his friends. Further, his situation between work and family was a contributing factor. This scenario covers a host of mistakes, any one of which alone could have negatively impacted on the opportunity. This $11 million loss, as I understand it, has become a standard barroom story that has amassed many new friends and relationships for the faltering investor. Maybe that's partial payback for him.

A "3" on the "Ugly Mistake Rating" is classified as catastrophic impact brought about by misjudgment, or assuming what should not simply be blindly counted upon. The scenario of this case study is a perfect fit.

CHAPTER 12

Learning from a Trifecta of My Miscalculations

"Failure is simply the opportunity to begin again, this time more intelligently"

—Henry Ford

To my credit, or discredit, these three ventures, early in my entrepreneurial journey, ultimately suffered from assumptions that were too aggressive or optimistic, and a severe case of me donning rose-colored glasses. They did not flourish as anticipated.

They are distinctive because they are "**foundation mistakes**," that is, each provided invaluable learning experiences that have served me well throughout my career, and my mentoring businesspeople.[4]

Russkie Brewskie was a brainchild of my days traveling to Russia to purchase titanium racing bicycle parts. Titanium was an inexpensive commodity in Russia, and labor was cheap (Figure 12.1).

On my free time, I made inroads with a Russian beer brewery but soon found out that Russian beer was inconsistent, atrocious, and not appropriate for the North American market. But the brand had appeal.

The concept of marketing Russian beer in North America would be a novel approach. After signing a Memorandum of Understanding with the Moscow-based brewery, the document itself could otherwise be described as a "Memorandum of Possible Vague Compliance" at best, we proceeded to find a brewery in the United States to license the line, since it was never our intent to actually produce it.

The promotional video was loaded with imagery, including Putin and Trump bare-chested on horseback, and other eye-catching Russian day-to-day glimpses which we found hilarious. Others did not.

---

[4]Photos are the property of the author, Jay Silverberg.

Figure 12.1 Russkie Brewskie was a politically motivated bottled beer brand

We had huge expectations. The U.S. brewery ran with Russkie Brewskie for several months, after which the public tired of it. We had made mistakes, all of which became learning curves.

International agreements are often iffy, and those signed with non-aligned countries are even iffier. Since then, I have every out-of-country agreement reviewed by my lawyers, not just theirs, and the final legal versions of agreements are in English. Further, our forecasts could have been tempered by more market research and more than "open bar night" at several locations where patrons imbibed with great gusto on any free beer with greater than 3 percent alcohol. Ours was 7 percent.

LESSONS LEARNED: A common piece of advice was to stay away from anything that invoked religious or political favoritism. We failed on all counts. We did almost recover our costs via royalties and license fees, but, alas, this brainchild never made it through kindergarten. Business "amusement" can carry a price tag.

Baby Boomer Reboot was an all-natural, certified supplement made with marine phytoplankton (Figure 12.2). The chemical makeup was conducive to help seniors deal with aches and pains and fill their nutritional needs with nature's own cure-all.

***Figure 12.2** Baby Boomer Reboot was a marine phytoplankton supplement for seniors*

We developed a strong alliance with research labs who condoned Baby Boomer Reboot. We also set up distribution with health food/supplement stores, and direct sales. All was great, until we got greedy.

We were approached by a promotion and distribution house based in Florida. Perhaps that, in itself, should have been a clue, but we were hungry for more and more.

This company professed to have strong ties with most major health product distributors and online merchants. All they needed was an exorbitant monthly retainer, and a warehouse full of our products. The projections were inspiring, and the deal was cut, too quickly, as it happened.

After prepaying the first six months retainer, the Florida agents virtually disappeared. No progress reports. Marginal sales at best. No forthcoming marketing campaign as promised, and, worst of all, broken lines of communication.

We went back to our original game plan and marketing strategy, doing everything ourselves, and achieved moderate success, licking our wounds along the retreat.

LESSONS LEARNED: The outcomes learned included; due more diligence with people you intend to do business with; trust your instincts; get all agreements with escape clauses whereby you can extricate yourself from bad deals.

Aq'Saak Aboriginal Foods was born as a giftware company producing Aboriginal teas and chocolate gifts, all beautifully packaged, including original artwork depicting the legends of the contributing tribes (Figure 12.3).

It was assumed that the cruise ships, tourist shops, and giftware boutiques would devour this novel line. It was, in fact, a magnificently packaged family of products.

All our original target markets preferred to keep hawking cheap Chinese-made souvenirs and gifts as opposed to supporting this regional initiative. We were devastated. Our assumptions bore little resemblance to our target markets and customer profiles.

Quickly we re-engineered our approach, but this time, our decisions were based on focus groups, direct contacts with potential buying groups, and an extensive campaign of sending samples and products as gifts.

Figure 12.3 AQ'SAAK *was a line of Indigenous-based teas*

Our new target customer base was museums, art shops, galleries, large department stores, and high-end only giftware retailers, preferably those with multiple locations.

LESSONS LEARNED: We had learned our lessons: When things go astray, don't be afraid to rethink your business model.

CHAPTER 13

The Best (or Worst) of the Worst Mistakes and Their Antidotes

"Each problem that I solved became a rule, which served afterwards to solve other problems."

—Rene Descartes

While we are never immune to mistakes in business, there are a number of blunders that you look at and decry "Of course, that makes sense," or "Why wouldn't (or would) entrepreneurs and managers do that?"

The following represent those kinds of mistakes, mostly from my own personal experience and from observing others whom I have mentored. Many represent learning curves or can become pathways to opportunities. Others, well, are just mistakes.

If you identify with any of the following missteps, self scrutiny of your approach to business may be appropriate.

PERHAPS YOU ARE SIMPLY TOO NICE. I often remind those whom I mentor that, not that I am intending to be unfeeling, but that employees are not family. They are paid staff and managers. That suggests maintaining a balance of openness and aloofness, a reasonable open-door policy, and an identifiable level of corporate hierarchy. Nobody should feel they have a direct line with "the boss" and can curry favors, because they will, and others will object, and it breeds discontent. It's human nature.

EMPLOYEES' PERSONAL LIVES. The more you involve yourself in the personal lives of your staff, the greater impact it will have on work-related decisions you may need to make. This would apply to anything, from promotions/demotions and responsibilities to changes in reporting structures. A sounder strategy is to maintain a professional and supportive approach without becoming overly involved in the personal lives of those around you.

GREED. The greater the greed factor, the faster you will act on opportunities without doing proper due diligence. You magically know it will work but have not arrived at a comfort level decision based on hard data and close examination. The only focus you may hold true is the prospect for profit. Greed is a mistake breeding ground.

RAISED EXPECTATIONS. This is a close kin of "greed." If your expectations for ROI (Return on Investment) are realistic and your return exceeds your prospects, then you will be pleasantly surprised and highly motivated to continue your pursuit. Conversely, should your results peak and fizzle out well below your hopes, chances are the venture will be abandoned, maybe prematurely, in search of the next shiny coin. Raised expectations have a low boiling point.

FALSE ASSUMPTIONS AS BUILDING BLOCKS. Common sense dictates that effective decision making is built on making assumptions based on fact. While motivation, enthusiasm, and personal interests enter into the process. Making the proper, fact-based decisions are the foundation. Market and industry research are often touted as critical. They deliver balance to whatever knee-jerk reactions you may normally harbor regarding opportunities and acting out on instinct. Rely on unblemished facts, current stats, and credible research results.

GOVERNANCE. The idea of setting work standards, performance milestones, and acceptable conduct is key. Everyone should know what is expected of them. This helps keep office and work routines on an even keel. Failing that, individuals tend to set their own levels and guidelines which can create tension and misperception within the company and allows divisions of responsibility to veer off course.

RESPONDING TO QUESTIONS. Experience has shown that responding to questions or "how do I?" should be encouraged. You are a natural resource for your team. However, the same inquiries over and over devour your own valuable time, distract you from your own tasks at hand, and is a red flag that the questioner has issues such as understanding their role, workload, and areas of responsibility. This is babysitting more than managing and needs to be dealt with. It may also reflect a lack confidence in their decision-making abilities. A level of independence on their part is important, for them and for you. If they are constantly concerned about making the wrong decision, they are of little use to your organization.

BOREDOM. Running out of steam. Losing interest. Faltering desire. Losing focus. Involvement burnout. Call it what you will. It happens, more so with start-up junkies who like to plan, build, and launch a business, but bore easily when it comes to running it long term. That's fine, but if you recognize this as a character trait you may have, then your planning should include an early exit strategy.

MAINTAINING GRUDGES. If there is one act that will come back to haunt you it's carrying bitterness and resentment. Feelings aside, unless it's an item with a significant dollar value or lost opportunity cost, learn to settle and let it go. The drain of unresolved issues on your focus can be dramatic and highly detrimental. Having experienced this with an employee who stole from me, I can attest that I wasted vast amounts of time and energy when any chance of recovery was questionable. I knew that but still persisted. My perspective has since become to let "Mother Nature deal with them." Chances are the perpetrators will continue their ways, ever increasing in boldness until they cross someone who will demand that justice be administered. Let the next victim settle the grudge.

CHANGE. This is one of the most feared words in business, OR, conversely, it is one of the most welcome shifts that your company can undergo. Whichever, it represents altering your course, good or bad. Your thinking needs to be ready and willing to consider the benefits and pitfalls of change, and adopting a mindset to act accordingly. Reacting to a changing market, be it adapting to new technologies or keeping pace with new industry players are cornerstone triggers for action. The key is "be ready." Brace yourself for the inevitable.

PERFORMANCE. Every team member in the business, even the owner and top managers, should be tracking their performance. Measuring output and deliverables in quantitative terms is key to assuring that whatever needs to get done is receiving the attention and priority that it merits. As well, when roles get periodically assessed, it is important to have a yardstick to measure past performance against.

YOUR SHORTCOMINGS. Nobody is perfect, but the ability to recognize our own limitations is important. Doing so quickly is equally imperative. You either accept these shortcomings as part of your makeup, and govern your performance to compensate, or you deal with them through training, mentoring, role modeling, counseling or serious introspection. Don't let your shortcomings dictate who you are and how others see you.

INSECURITY LEADS TO IMMOBILIZATION. A common issue for businesspeople is wavering, that is, uncertainty leading to delays or half-hearted implementation of ideas or action. The cure is research and carrying out due diligence in order to gain the confidence you need to move forward. Quite often, opportunities wait for no one, and hesitation is a byproduct of the error of allowing insecurity to overshadow your decision making.

STATS AND MORE STATS. Situations often arise where information, hard data, and reports are prominent tools you need to make decisions. However, there is a danger in oversaturation whereby stats are never enough to provide you with the impetus to take action. You hunger for more. You need greater clarification. Your comfort level has not yet been reached, possibly never. The danger here is that regardless of what masses of intelligence you assemble, it's never enough. Insecurity comes into play. Perhaps this is an indicator in itself for you not to proceed. Or learn to adopt an attitude of "better not best," and assuming you may never have that last piece of information that tops you up. Either act or move on to the next pressing issue.

FLOGGING A DEAD HORSE. Ideas and opportunities have an inherent lifespan, and delays slowly shut the passageway to owning the prospect. The same principle applies to mistakes. Striving to correct a mistake by dancing around various wannabe solutions only exacerbates the blunder. Whatever you have in front of you, it is imperative to be decisive and not simply consider halfway measures.

DELEGATE. Although we entrepreneurs often consider ourselves as invincible and tireless multitaskers, the truth is that the more we take on, the weaker our performance on the host of tasks and responsibilities burdening our shoulders. Find the right people to delegate to, and, if insecurity still makes you nervous, establish a process of spot checking/micromanaging those to whom you have delegated part of your load. In the same vein, it may make sense to seek the help of an uninvolved third party to help sort out the details of a new division of responsibility within your organization.

PROTECTING IP. Far too often companies ignore the need to safely cocoon their IP which is such an important part of a company's capital. Never take it for granted that your IP protection is invincible. There are always loopholes, and newcomers trying to wedge their way in. Make no mistake. Review the security of your IP annually.

BEING PERFECT. This concept is often an untenable, out of reach expectation. It also kills good ideas and/or inflames mistakes. Come to the realization that we are flawed. "Almost perfect" or simply reaching out toward the light is often good enough.

SCALING UP, OR SCALING BACK. Doing either changes the course of your business. Acting on emotion or fear or adrenalin all represent the wrong triggers. Key decisions demand a mindset free of diversions that often color your response or adversely impact your reaction time.

COMPARING YOURSELF TO OTHERS. We are who we are. Comparing yourself to industry "stars" is a futile exercise. The only thing you should learn is that these stratosphere dwellers are people too, and their greatest virtue may be, aside from wealth and power, is that they have discovered how to camouflage their weaknesses. You are who you are, and it has likely allowed you to achieve your current level of success. Stick with the game plan.

TOO GOOD TO BE TRUE. It is likely not true. Objectivity is an important perspective to maintain, although it is often not easy when you are staring at what could be an unimaginable score. Learn to take a step back to survey the opportunity. Rushing to grasp the golden ring can lead to painful slips. Others' excitement can also get you excited. Realizing that will bring greater calmness to the prospect at hand. Ask yourself some tough questions rather than taking everything (or anything) at face value.

TRUST. Only trust people when you have proof of their trustworthiness. Don't trust online testimonials. They can be quite creative or AI generated. Trust references from customers directly and ask to also speak with those who had negative outcomes. There's a lot to be learned from both extremities of the scale.

ACCOUNTABILITY. Clever people still make dumb decisions. Mediocre businesspeople make even more faux pas, some quite costly. Hold everyone, including your team, accountable for their actions and decisions. You decide on the sanctions, but remember, nobody, not even you, is always perfect.

YOUR TO DO LIST. Assume you will never tick off all the items before new ones get added. The shortsightedness here is if and when you de-prioritize the important, more urgent "to-dos" in favor of what interests you the most, stuff will fall through the cracks.

INSTANT SATISFACTION IS WISHFUL THINKING. We all want results, and the more exciting the possibilities, the faster we want them. This applies to just about anything; investments, market forays, acquisitions, de-acquisitions, and hiring high-fliers, among other acts of great anticipation. Patience in business is not necessarily a virtue, but neither is jumping off a cliff in rabid excitement.

ACCOUNTANTS, LAWYERS, AND CONSULTANTS. These professionals are businesspeople who dispense advice and counsel, all of which is fine, but they are third party, uninvolved players who earn a living off you. They may be friendly but are generally not your close friends. You are their client, and they will have many clients with varying needs, interests, and concerns. The mistake many entrepreneurs make is that they seem to think that any recommendations offered by these sources are gospel, when they are not necessarily so. Understand their roles and their usefulness. Use them as sounding boards if you like, but don't live solely by their feedback.

This is a snapshot of a prepaid phone card fiasco before my company took on the mandate to assist in their restructuring.

The client was one of the first, major telephone prepaid card suppliers, primarily for the private sector, including universities, private schools, corporations, and government. All cards were customized in terms of design and pricing. At the time, the client was earning about $6 million per year in revenues, and growing by 20 percent annually, with a healthy bottom line and a loyal client base. Competition was scattered, with few rivals matching my clients' performance and market share.

So, what could have possibly been wrong?

Firstly, they were investing heavily in new servers and long-term contracts with communications providers. It was evident from our market research that the phone cards business was being leapfrogged by advanced cellphone services and providers and the sector was shortly to go into a massive decline. It was becoming obsolete.

The founders refused to accept this premise. Their greed was a naive error in judgment, coupled with a refusal to accept forthcoming legal and regulatory changes debuting in the marketplace.

In a bid to salvage the phone card industry, the service providers from whom my client was buying bulk long-distance time, were slashing their prices to all newcomers and selling directly to the public to protect what dwindling markets were still available. The impact on my client was devastating.

Our suggestions were based on salvaging what we could; terminate contracts with suppliers who had become competitors; cancel all contracts for equipment upgrades and other capital expenditures not yet consummated, and; pursue a niche market that still demanded prepaid phone cards. That was the immigrant/newcomer market, unable to get credit for cellphones and other long-distance services, and who still bought cards at local corner grocery stores, mostly for calling home overseas.

Our clients soon realized the error of their ways.

- Arrogance in assuming the market still had "legs" and was growing, which it was not. The increases in their revenues were really attributable to competitors fleeing the rapidly declining marketplace.
- The face of a rapidly changing technology marketplace rendering their service almost obsolete.
- Competition from their very own bulk time suppliers, which was a sure sign of a quickly collapsing market.

Yet our client was prepared to march blindly into the abyss.

Our implemented strategies worked for a while, but we all knew these were short-term survival tactics to plan the least painful exit for our client.

Score	Good Mistake Rating	Bad Mistake Rating	Ugly Mistake Rating
3			
2			
1			

Lesson(s) Learned: Mistakes are your capital only if you pay attention and read the tea leaves. In this case, a combination of blunders regarding the market, changing technology, and other crucial evidence was ignored. Disbelief reigned. Blinders created a shortsighted view of the future, and drastic action was needed to take place to salvage what they could. In the long run, they were fortunate to have connected with us and, more importantly, wise enough to listen to us when we demonstrated the limited options they had. It was a valuable short-term salvaging pivot.

A "3" rating as an "Ugly Mistake" is deserved when, as in this case, a major shift in the marketplace is foreseen but does not elicit a change in how the business operates. In this case, a series of challenges were painfully obvious, including deep-discount competition, how technology was changing the delivery of services, and even regulatory issues. All roadblocks stared the company in the face. Disbelief reigned. Disaster was inevitable unless a dramatic pivot was launched.

CHAPTER 14

Ego Clouds Decision Making and Causes Mistakes

"It's good to learn from your mistakes. It's better to learn from other people's mistakes."

—Warren Buffett

Ego is a mask. It is deceitful, to ourselves and to others. Its skewed perspective often leads to making poor choices, or being oblivious to red flags, or awaiting opportunities. What should be apparent, but is too often blinded by ego, is a precursor to errors in judgment or blatant omission.

- Ego feeds on personal priorities, often at odds with what is best for the business.
- Ego is a weakness that your competitors will weaponize and use against you.
- Ego generates its own perspectives, offering up personal rather than corporate viewpoints. It is often a narrow focus on life, or a shortfall of personal skills.
- Ego's growth mindset is singular and does not generally encompass the growth and betterment of those around it.
- Ego breeds entitlement, deserved or otherwise.
- Ego's principal feature is an abundance of overconfidence, warranted or not.
- Ego is often shamefully prideful and boastful in a way that annoys those around them.
- Ego demands respect and subservience, even and especially where that comes from power instead of performance.
- Egotistical leaders are often isolationists. After all, what could others possibly contribute other than obedience?

- Ego is often the sole source of opinion and ideas to resolve issues. Feedback is unwelcome or accepted in a condescending manner. After all, who knows better?
- Ego tends to respond in a knee-jerk fashion. Answers, right or wrong, to almost everything are spontaneous. Acting too fast instigated by ego can make them lose even faster.
- Ego is not a collaborator or team player, unless they hold the deciding vote, frequently regardless of the experience, knowledge base or views of others. You really don't need to solve *every* problem yourself.
- Ego's prime goals are self-aggrandizement and self-preservation, both equally destructive and detrimental in managing a business.

Ego and Leadership

- Leaders with strong egos are often not leaders, but dictators.
- Decision-making skills are not guaranteed qualities of leaders. In fact, it is often the reverse.
- Ego leadership style is not conducive to generating a team spirit. The working environment is often quite toxic with distressed and fearful managers and staff cowering, kowtowing, and offering disingenuous support to protect their employment based on intimidation. That is the lowest form of job engagement.
- Ego-driven leaders are resistant to change or even consider change unless it is aligned with their personal goals and expectations. For example, deciding to dramatically increase top management salaries and bonuses when the company is struggling is a clear indication of a business run by an egomaniac with little or no sensitivity to market perception or the interests of the company's shareholders or customers.
- Acknowledging failure and mistakes is not part of an ego persona. That avoidance just breeds more mistakes, some attributable to unresolved blunders.
- When an ego-driven business owner or upper tier manager uses pride instead of sensible reasoning or emotion instead of logic, the mistakes at hand are exacerbated and continue to inflict harm on many levels.

- One of the worst features of ego-driven leaders or top managers is the inability or unwillingness to recognize challenges and upcoming pressing issues that need to be addressed or are already swirling around the business' foothold and existence. This can be analogous to the story of Nero fiddling while Rome burned. Now *there* was an egomaniac in power!

Ego and Decision Making

- A strong ego is often a biased ego, and that can follow through to decisions made on personal or even biased assumptions.
- Inflated egos are steeped in overconfidence and can generate inappropriate decisions and outcomes.
- The opinions offered by others are often downplayed and viable solutions to problems ignored.
- Solid decisions are based on research and due diligence. Egocentric decision makers tend to limit these input sources.
- Laying blame on others is a feature of ego-driven businesspeople, especially when they themselves fail to admit mistakes. This creates an atmosphere of insecurity and fear of reprisal within an organization, almost to the level of toxicity.
- The bottom line is that ego can negatively impact the business's profits, and that alone sums up the inherent damage that ego-driven founders, managers, key employees, and investors/stakeholders can generate. Personal agendas get in the way of profit.

If you recognize anything in the preceding about your own personal style and leadership habits, perhaps it is time for introspection and refocusing your efforts, outlook, and style in order for you to become more of an open-minded and receptive team player.

That's enough about the darker side. Let's look at how ego in business can deliver better decision making and far fewer painful and shortsighted lapses.

- There is a place for ego in displaying and "oozing" confidence in crisis situations or adopting a leadership role where group consensus is vital. Try to be an open-minded leader of the pack.

- Respect feedback. You don't always need to be right.
- Ego-focused leaders, owners, and managers tend to be resistant to learning. Don't be. Every learning experience is an opportunity to grow.
- If people cower in your presence, their value to the company is marginalized. Bullying is not an appropriate management tool. Keep your ego in check.
- Fostering an immovable ego can stunt your growth, both personal and professional, and disrespects all feedback. Learn to listen.
- Your way of doing things is not the only way. Different is not analogous to "wrong." Be open to others.
- Delegate instead of hoarding and/or trying to multitask, well, just about everything. There are others close to you with talent, albeit maybe not operating at your level, but certainly good enough to be capable to proffer advice and counsel and act on your behalf.
- You don't need to know everything.
- **Acknowledge your people. Respect them. Remember why you hired them, what skills you saw in them.** Use their skills wisely.
- Commit to learn, including from those around you. Everything becomes a learning experience and everyone you deal with is a teacher/mentor to a certain degree.

Living in an ego-free business or corporate environment is impossible. In fact, ego is an important survival skill. The issue is when "over-ego" clouds your judgment, your decision making and your ability to effectively interact with your support people. Then it makes you ineffective. A burden more than a valuable asset to the business. A liability rather than capital.

Work on changing to let others get close to you. Acceptance, recognition of others, and less reliance on the roadblocks that ego erects will give you more resilience to lean on as a leader and less of an invincible "lead superstar's" play acting role.

Our client, an outdoors adventure TV series, had just negotiated and signed a broadcast agreement with one of China's smaller networks with a viewership of 480 million. Smaller indeed by Chinese standards.

They were excited beyond belief, and assumed a partnership with a giant, respected broadcaster was totally legitimate and the agreement reflected everything all parties had agreed to.

As the relationship was ready for launch, my clients had a foreboding hindsight uneasy feeling about their contracted obligations and profit-sharing formulas. We were engaged in a type of postmortem due diligence, a strange position to be in.

The agreement they signed, that is the legal version, was in Mandarin. My client had a nonbinding English translation. The two, as it turned out, were different, with the Mandarin version being distinctly in the Chinese partners' favor.

Having lived through something similar before, I had the Mandarin version translated by two independent sources. We identified several troubling key clauses where the Mandarin version was different, and we raised the issues with all stakeholders.

Our client had planned to sign North American resort advertisers to attract a growing Chinese affluent middle-class keen to travel outside China. The agreement, however, stated that the Chinese partner had to abide by The Peoples Republic of China's Ministry of Propaganda and the shows' advertising spots could not all be sold to western concerns. Our clients' potential earnings sank underwater.

I was given the dubious task of trying to change the Ministry's ruling. Nobody else on our team wanted this responsibility.

In inimitable Chinese fashion of the time, it took a vast amount of networking, socializing, showing respect, entertaining and opulent gift exchanges to amend this ruling to allow our client a greater window of opportunity. And I convinced the Ministry and the network to assume the final broadcast translations, editing and promotion of the series with minimal exposure to my client.

This was not ideal, but workable.

The show lasted one year on the air in China. The relationship was never quite as mutual as was originally intended. Suspicion reigned. But, at least, our client survived and profited from the publicity as the first of its kind to win broadcast rights in China, a reputation that served them well in their North American forays.

Score	Good Mistake Rating	Bad Mistake Rating	Ugly Mistake Rating
3			
2			
1			

Lesson(s) Learned: Trust must be earned, not assumed. It is your capital that you are offering up, and do not do so willingly or without assessing the implications if things were to go sideways. Further, the excitement of most deals has a kernel of adversity or ambiguity. Be cautious before jumping in blinded with a euphoric state. Think of all the possible "what ifs."

Our client found themselves involved in an exceptional opportunity but enmeshed in a situation that presented a complex downside. Recognizing their precarious position, they took action to better their position in the alliance with their Chinese partner. This warrants a "2" in the "Good Mistake Rating" chart. The company faced a serious obstacle and dealt with it as best they could, and enjoyed a reasonable outcome.

CHAPTER 15

Your Business Vision Is Your Brand

"Ideas are easy. Execution is everything."

—John Doerr

A business vision tells your marketplace, your customers, and the world what your long-term aspirations are, how you want others to appreciate you, recognize you, and buy into your core values, where you are going, and why you have chosen that pathway.

Treat it with respect, and it will do likewise, and reward you. Treat it with disdain and that business mistake will haunt you.

Your brand vision is more so a personal qualitative statement of how you see yourself and allowing others to peek into your business life-space.

Good visioning statements are carefully crafted. Few words. Huge imagery and meaning. Easily translatable and decipherable by all. You build your business around your aspirations.

Here are a few recognizable examples. They originate from Google, Tesla, Amazon, and Starbucks. Try to match them up.

- "To accelerate the world's transition to sustainable energy."
- "To be the earth's most customer-centric company where customers can find and discover anything they might want to buy online."
- "To inspire and nurture the human spirit—one person, one cup, one neighborhood at a time."
- "To provide access to the world's information in one click."

These are all excellent branding vision statements. They inspire, direct the reader to their future, encompass eventualities without over glorifying or even being specific in nature. They have impact, are memorable, and are readily attributable to the corporate entity.

What features do bad brand vision statements exhibit?

- Unrealistic, such as this direct quote "We will own 75% the market within six months."
- Contain tired buzzwords such as "solutions, innovative, and leader."
- Wrong target audience, as in "creating value for shareholders" when the brand/outreach customer focus needs to be on the marketplace that buys from you and meeting buyers' needs.
- Uses words where the customer assumes the reverse is true. Words such as "honest, valuable, high-quality, and dependable."
- Generic and uninspiring phrases that are anything but memorable, such as "Striving to be the best. (Does that mean you are currently the 'worst'?)"
- Tries to please everyone by making broadside statements that generally fall short of the mark, pleasing few or none.
- Lies, such as promising health-conscious results while selling highly processed triple burgers, shakes, and deep-fried snacks. Honesty is tossed out the door.
- When brand vision statements focus more on the company than on the clients, it begs the question "why bother?"

A solid, simple, understandable statement creates opportunities when it creates an emotion or touches on the needs and expectations of the customer. It helps to solidify your market position and supports the brand you have designed to entice business.

Conversely, a poorly thought-out statement is ignored, at best, or ridiculed, at worst, and acts as a reputational/ image deterrent instead of an attractant.

Visualize a workable, fine-tuned brand vision statement as the positive polarity of a magnet and the less meaningful, forgettable statement as the negative or repulsing polarity of a magnet.

Key Takeaway Considerations in Formulating a Great Brand Vision Statement

To ensure you avoid mistakes that can cost you, there are a number of safeguards and steps you can consider to arrive at a positive brand vision statement outcome. Ask yourself:

- Does this statement properly represent who we are, or is it just a way to cloak ourselves in a "feel good" envelope?
- Does every person (or most of the team) in the company buy into this statement?
- Does it exhibit future-forward thinking?
- Are any statements or phrases we use likely to be obsolete within a short timeframe? Are we staying current?
- Is our outreach targeted for the marketplace, that is, our client base?
- Are our stated goals realistic and achievable? Attainable but not yet attained?
- Does it reflect our passion to perform and deliver?
- Can any statements made be deemed somewhat of a far distant and difficult to achieve daydream that can come back and bite us?
- Can this brand vision statement be translated into daily action and attitude among our people?

The Rocket Ship Coffee House (pseudonym) was intended as a quirky, high-octane coffee house catering to a niche market for serious coffee connoisseurs tired of the chains churning out concoctions that barely resembled coffee.

Rocket was intended for purists, from specialized coffee bean sourcing and roasting to serving coffee with enough caffeine to get your nerves jangling.

This was intended as the flagship, the first of many planned locations. The marketing needed to have as much punch as their coffee and their other caffeine-laced delicacies.

The founders were eager to create a gritty corporate vision statement that would best reflect who they were and what they intended to do, and to do so from a niche customer's perspective. The direction was to be carried through to their marketing and branding, as is often the case.

My suggestions included the following. These were likely helped by several servings of their potent and awesome brew. This Rocket mandate we were contracted to deliver was exceptionally enjoyable, from the open-minded founders to the creative freedom that allowed us to break the rules.

- **Brand Vision**: Rediscover coffee. Wicked high-octane coffee brewers for dedicated and discriminating coffee lovers.
- **Goal**: The Red Bull of Coffee
- **Suggested Product Names**: "Never Blink Again Java," "Near Death by Coffee," "Better Than Sex Brand Coffee," "Rocket Fuel Coffee," "Banned Coffee Blend."

Rocket's critical visioning error was assuming they would be a great coffee provider, but without anything distinctive about themselves. To better differentiate themselves from a crowded coffee market, everything about Rocket needed to be a cross between very avant guard and goth light. That was our primary recommendation.

Score	Good Mistake Rating	Bad Mistake Rating	Ugly Mistake Rating
3			
2			
1			

Lesson(s) Learned: The brand vision statement exemplified exactly who they were, what their market niche was, and what would appeal to their customer base. Their perspective was integrated into everything they did, from branding their coffee names, coffee house décor, and a staff immersed into their religious zeal. Rocket's brand vision statement was their capital, and it was meaningful, opportunistic, and effective. With our creative intervention, they made no mistake in pinpointing exactly what they were about and who they meant to serve.

The business was built on a solid foundation, but demanded repositioning/rebranding to capture its intended market. Ideas and concepts were presented and accepted, and the business succeeded. This scenario represents a "3" in the "Good Mistake Rating" chart, namely offering up a pathway to opportunities not part of the company's current products, but accepted and integrated into its operation.

CHAPTER 16

Business Model Mistakes and Solutions

"Success is not final. Failure is not fatal. It is the courage to continue that counts."

—Winston Churchill

The business model you conform to takes into account three critical factors:

1. How quickly can you monetize your services or generate revenues from your products?
2. How rapidly can you build a base of repeat customers, multiple revenue streams or a significant following on social media or through online sales?
3. Which business model reflects the nature of your business and provides the best avenues to penetrate the market and position yourself among or ahead of your competitors?

These are the most often-used business models. Where does your business fit in, and why would that be your most effective model to meet all three criteria listed above?

Model	Description	Strengths	Weaknesses
Direct-to-Consumer (D2C)	The most common model with sales direct to consumers through a web-based catalog of products such as Amazon	Builds a direct relationship with customers and a database of buyers	Building trust is a big factor. Customer service needs to be exceptional.
Business-to-Business (B2B)	Online and direct sales to businesses, and delivery of supplies and services	Can represent recurring and repeat/scheduled orders	Often based more so on price and is a competitive environment

(continued)

Model	Description	Strengths	Weaknesses
Fees-Based Services	Hourly, daily, retainer fee structure most often refers to consulting or contracted expertise or virtual employees	Attempts to control costs via an "engage as you need" model	Customer service and value for services are key, and contracted lifespan is often limited
Subscription	Service provided based on a monthly membership fee, such as newsletter services or Netflix or Google Drive Storage or iCloud	Predictable and regular revenue stream	Membership fluctuations and providers promoting costly upgrades
Free Subscriptions	As above, users access a base service for free but there is an upcharge for premium services such as Zoom	Can represent rapid client base	Membership is tentative and turnover is commonplace
On Demand Model	Promises to deliver immediate goods or services such as Uber	Based on convenience, speed of service and lower costs	Strengths can be their weakness. Highly competitive.
Transactional Model	Customers access this model to purchase a specific product, generally a one-time transaction such as Apple	Has the ability to connect with buyers and build a database for future sales	Based moreso on single transactions, repeat business demands post sales marketing and database upkeep

Common Errors in Business Model Selection

The following blunders can seriously influence your business model.

- Assuming models such as subscriptions and membership will have sufficient appeal so as to encourage uptakes and signups
- Pricing too high discourages customers, while, conversely, low pricing generates suspicion among potential buyers, especially for products where knock-offs prevail. Pricing is a balancing act.
- Underservicing the client base, including "iffy" customer service, makes for a short-term relationship

- Competition plays leapfrog, with new competitors continually entering the marketplace, many employing more sophisticated technology, and clawing for precious market share. Vigilance is key.
- Cash flow, both for start-ups and companies in the process of building out or on their business model, is the fuel for growth. It is often wrongly assumed that revenue alone will support all the fluctuations that any business will likely endure.
- Reputation and brand recognition/loyalty are the foundation of any business model. Any deterioration, for whatever cause, needs to be avoided or gaffes dealt with fast, especially in the eyes of the firm's client base, and the business' marketplace in general.
- Delivery channels change. Yours may be slower, costlier or less responsive. Find out.
- Overreaching such as targeting a large demographic pool, a substantial geographic/regional focus. Too vast a products or services offering can also be unmanageable.
- Your final measure is your bottom line. Stay on top of your returns (EBITDA). A dramatic shift may also be cause to revisit or revamp your current business model.

How Business Model Mistakes Become Business Opportunities

1. Either at the start-up of your business, or anywhere along its journey when a revisit is useful, define your Value Proposition. Assure yourself that you are meeting the needs of the client base and community and that there is an identifiable need for what you are bringing to market.
2. Understand your market. It changes continuously, and you must change with it to accommodate. Never stop researching, and that includes scouting new competitors and revisiting existing ones.
3. Delivering value often boils down to pricing and costs. Stay uber-competitive.

4. Demographics shift. Buying groups change. Stay in close touch with your customers, especially the 2 percent that provide 80 percent of your revenues. That's a proven statistic.
5. Know your typical customer. People who inhabit your customer niche are your target. Keep defining or redefining who supports you. Covet them. Go the extra mile.
6. Assure that your business model is still effective. Test it. Tweak or shift it if necessary. The flood of businesses that have embraced online sales is an example of "change or die." For example, Walmart's online sales have grown by 25 percent, representing five times its increase in instore-sales growth numbers.[5]
7. Learn to adapt. Change is not a bad thing. Flexibility is ultimately rewarding.

An early client of mine, SpecTV (pseudonym), had a daydream to become the number one supplier of in-room video rentals in hotels throughout the southern United States, including Florida. This was a growing marketplace where, at the time, cable boxes were still used to access entertainment of all sorts, including on demand videos.

The market was dominated by a major player with strong ties to hotels as well as affiliations with content providers. This did not deter SpecTV. There was a stubborn arrogance among the founders who, themselves, had only marginal experience in the sector.

In an industry where license and royalty payments to both entertainment providers and hotels were a mainstay of doing business, SpecTV was quickly depleting their cash.

We were brought in to help find investors or partners.

We declined the mandate until the company proved themselves to us. At face value, based on the information and plans provided, we felt that there was not enough substance to excite other stakeholders. However, we agreed to stay involved for a while as we did our own due diligence and got to know their team.

[5]https://www.digitalcommerce360.com/article/walmart-online-sales/#.

They had issues.

- The founding group was more interested in the investment side than in the actual service delivery they were promoting. SpecTV was an investment opportunity more than a serious services provider.
- Marginally experienced technology staffers were learning about the sector's needs and deliverable venues even as they programmed, almost by braille. Catch-up technology expertise was not a salable feature of the company.
- A disjointed Business Plan that was more wishful thinking than strategic planning.
- A proforma budget that, in our opinion, was overly aggressive at best and entirely unrealistic at worst. It was drafted as a selling document for investors seeking a high return-high turnaround, and less about abilities to deliver results to users. Market penetration was a pipedream.
- Risk received only minimal attention.

The worst aspect of SpecTV was their business-to-business model. Their appeal, as they saw it, was to attract hotel venues with expensive future licensing fees, but doing so, without having too many credible entertainment providers secured as of yet. Their entire start-up focus was getting cable boxes into the hotel suites. The hotels did not buy into this model.

As well, the industry, dominated by a couple of well-branded competitors, would not allow a newcomer to establish a toehold. They had programming options and new and even more upcoming technology that SpecTV was years away from being able to offer.

Again, undeterred, SpecTV continued on its course. The gap between themselves and their successful competitors widened. Their cash burn rate caught up to them.

As for their business model, if they had started with a business-to-consumer (B2C) model and worked to secure a foothold in a restricted and more controllable regional marketplace, they might have been able to garner a key but limited client base. This was our suggestion, including launching in a beta region where any glitches in their technology or service delivery would not be fatal.

They soldiered on without us, without heeding our recommendations. They were committed to a business model more so to attract capital rather than becoming a serious industry contender, which seemed to be a secondary, albeit vital goal.

They ceased to exist when their last dollar was spent.

Score	Good Mistake Rating	Bad Mistake Rating	Ugly Mistake Rating
3			
2			
1			

Lesson(s) Learned: Forgoing an opportunity to redeem themselves by changing course to a more realizable business model was fatal. Furthermore, a business needs to question its core motives. In SpecTV's case, securing investors and partners was uppermost in their aspirations. This alone contributed to the demise of the company. It wasn't just the haughty goals as much as them pursuing an unattainable business model where being a real player demanded big money and even bigger connections, neither of which SpecTV had, or was capable of securing, especially with a narrowly focused and wishful thinking team.

SpecTV's focus on investors rather than developing marketable services was a fatal mistake, a misjudgment that put the company onto an inalterable pathway to oblivion. A "3" Ugly Mistake Rating was warranted and rightfully earned. The company did not recognize its suicidal behavior.

CHAPTER 17

Avoiding Partnership Misunderstandings

"Individually we are one drop, but together we are an ocean,"

—Ryunosuke Satoro

After the hostile breakup of my second partnership, my ex-partner had a heart attack, not, I might add, brought about by me. Perhaps it was induced by his third (or fourth?) wife, a younger version of himself, but far smarter and even more painfully self-centered.

I felt a shallow pang of remorse when I heard about his heart attack and had not reached out to him to express my sympathies, so I gathered myself up, proceeded to a greeting card store, and wandered looking for the most appropriate message card.

A salesclerk approached me and offered her help. I replied, "I am looking for a get-well card for someone I don't really care about and with a message I don't genuinely mean." She wandered away, rolling her eyes, never to be seen in my presence again.

Such is the good news-bad news imagery of a partnership. It can work incredibly well, or it can be soul-destroying.

It can build your business, working together, or shred it as the partnership immerses you in uncharted shark-infested territory.

Questions to Ask Yourself Before Partnering

1. Do you need a partner, and why?
2. What do you expect out of a partner? Funding? Work and responsibility sharing? Access to other opportunities? Access to their clients and markets?
3. If your partnership is based primarily on funding, what happens when the money runs out, and it will? What then?

4. Have you done your due diligence on the partner prospects? References? Past successes?
5. Partnership means ceding power. How much are you willing to share?
6. Is there a personality and ethical match? Do you share values? If not, the funders' money is not enough to make it work.

The Partnership Courtship Dance

The creation of a partnership goes through several distinct stages of evolution.

1. The **chase and courtship** where both parties fluff themselves up, aggrandize their assets and abilities, and embrace. It's a tender moment of great anticipation.
2. The **living together trial**. Let's see how we get along but without any legal commitments. Possibly a memorandum or nonbinding letter of interest or intent.
3. If everything works as planned, the union ensues with a **partnership agreement (PA)**. Here is where self-interest comes into play. The PA is a legal agreement with clauses to safeguard each party's interests. It needs to be clear as to financial considerations, division of responsibility, decision making, and breakup/termination spelled out in advance. It also needs to be enforceable by either party, with due consideration to the partner with less financial resources to defend themselves. Proceed with caution. Hire your own contract adviser. An escape clause is highly recommended.
4. The **honeymoon** follows. It is similar to the courting but there is an aura of the newness of the relationship based on what each had promised to deliver via the PA. Enjoy the cautious jubilance.
5. Everything works as expected. Or it does not. After some time, you've **grown apart**, or one of you has lost interest, or moved onto the next shiny coin. It is now that the PA's termination and succession clauses shine. You have protected yourself, right?

The perfect partnership model is one that works for you both. Your abilities may be on different levels, but you share a common interest in making the company succeed. Most importantly, there is a **synergy** between you where the sum of both of your talents put into play together, exceeds the sum total of you both individually. This goes well beyond "strength in numbers." It implies **symbiosis**.

A smoothly functioning partnership, or even one that has been salvaged and reworked, as often happens, represents an opportunity to succeed. Fixing bruised partnership mistakes is your capital, your harmony, your synergy.

Pros and Cons of a Partnership

Most often occurring features of a partnership are presented herein depicting the pros and cons for each feature of a working partnership.

Pros of a Partnership	Cons of a Partnerships
Shared liability	Becomes an issue when one partner has greater cash resources than the other
Sharing of common perspectives and goals	One party can become unfocused on the business, distracted by other opportunities and contribute less to the prime enterprise
Shared ethics, scruples, morals and values	Comfortable with flexible ethics[6] that go against core beliefs. Conflicts arise.
Less financial burden	Only until the partner's investments are spent
Collaborative decision making	Conflicts arise when consensus is not achieved. Inaction can often result in a stalemate.
Autonomy rests with you, the sole shareholder	Loss of autonomy, and potential growth and change can be stifled
Profits belong to you	Profits shared with partner(s)
Greater resources and management sharing	New division of responsibilities can cause you to micromanage the other partner
Go into business with a friend	Lose a friend

[6] "The business universe is often characterized by its own rules, (purported) ethics, morals, scruples, intents, and operating principles. While they are portrayed and taught as cast in stone, in reality, they are not. The real world of entrepreneurship revolves around "survive–grow–adapt–succeed," and that absolutely gives the businessperson the opportunity to flex these norms to their own needs, always looking out for what is best for themselves." *A Cynic's Business Wisdom: Winning through Flexible Ethics, Business Expert Press, 2021. Author, Jay Silverberg.*

Having said that, there are danger signals that are broadcast. It is imperative that you remain vigilant to any of these. Here are the most telling ones.

- If and when the relative contributions of each partner become imbalanced
- Disagreements that cause antagonism between parties
- Diminished focus where other ventures and opportunities distract one of the partners
- Flexible ethics take on an overreaching tone
- Capital expenditures are frowned upon by one or the other. Opinions vary.
- Untoward behavior making decisions such as undertaking planning without you. Possibly secrecy prevails.
- A shift in attitude where blame only flows one way. Toward you.

Building on the Strength and Capital of a Partnership

- Remain attentive to any changes that wander away from the original Agreement and overriding understanding and intent of the partnership.
- Be cautious of the benefits, risks, and expectations of a partnership. Don't open yourself up to being blindsided.
- Resolve issues as they arise and do so quickly and in everyone's mutual interest.
- The division of responsibility is cast until both parties agree to change it.
- Keep each partner accountable for their areas of responsibility and performance.
- Build on mutual reliance and commitment. These are unwavering features of a workable partnership.
- Don't expect perfection. Nobody will ever meet your standards.
- Any serious falling-out, or the near-term advent of same, plan your exit strategy. Refer to your Agreement and understand the process. Protect and prepare yourself.

I was always a strong believer in partnerships; share the load, work in unison, synergistic capabilities, greater resources, and so on. All the theoretical goodies that partners provide, like a warm blanket on a cold day.

Somehow, I missed the boat. I have had a number of partners. A couple were reasonably okay, one was invisible, and the others were "meh." It's only recently since I have been analyzing and writing about partners and partnerships that I appreciate what I did right, and what I did wrong.

There are two truths I discovered about myself regarding partners.

1. I am big on trust. So much so that I believed almost everything that I heard in partnership discussions, and when key promises were not delivered, such as investment envelopes, industry contacts, and equal workload undertakings, it was too late. The damage became ingrained in the relationship, with a troubled road ahead of us facing a pending divorce.
2. I am an enthusiastic person. This is one of the characteristics of the "start-up junkie" who is captured and captivated by a promising venture or growth scenario. The result was that, even when I began to see the partnership unravel around the edges, I still maintained a positive attitude. "It will work out. Give it time." Time ran out. Adversarial issues were left alone to breed and bleed out.

A prime example was my last partner. Promises mostly unfulfilled. Joint decision making that was mostly disjointed. Apparently, we lived on different planets. Grandiose plans all of which included him spending mostly my money, and when I declined further cash injections, things got much worse.

Good turned ugly, but it was fixable. I purchased his shares, dusted off my ego, re-energized, and became a far better entrepreneur without ever looking back. My mistake was a costly learning experience. My capital.

Score	Good Mistake Rating	Bad Mistake Rating	Ugly Mistake Rating
3			
2			
1			

Lesson(s) Learned: I learned some valuable lessons in the process.

- Don't mix personal and business relationships.
- Tough partnership times make you stronger. I became a much more confident decision maker and manager. That was a gift that partnerships gave me.
- Protect yourself. Tie up the other party. Remove any contractual wiggle room.
- Set definable deliverables/expectations and milestones for your partner that, if not delivered, catapults accountability to the forefront.
- Build on solid partnerships. They certainly do exist.
- Walk (or run) away from any festering ones at the first sign of trouble.

The rating of "3" as a "Bad Mistake" was aptly earned. Perhaps I was oblivious to my last partners' character flaws during the honeymoon stage of the relationship, but the "shiny coin on the road" may have impeded my flight reflex. The saving grace was that, as problems manifested the relationship, they were identified and dealt with in a judicious fashion in time to protect my interests.

CHAPTER 18

Understanding the Business Plan: Mistakes, Impact, and Opportunities

"A goal without a plan is just a wish."

—Antoine De Saint-Exupéry

A Business Plan is simply an expression of where you want to go, how you will get there, and what awaits you when you arrive.

It is a customized document created for a specific readership: funders, investors, partners, and/or, of course for you as a roadmap. And it is alive, adapting to changing markets, technologies, opportunities, and new-found ideas and strategies that may drive your enterprise.

It is a snapshot that is current and accurate only on the day it is completed, and open to change anytime thereafter. How old is your current Business Plan? Is it still relevant? Does it reflect who you are today?

The Effective Business Plan Encompasses Seven Distinct Features

1. Goal oriented, with a purposeful vision and mission statement very clear to the reader(s).
2. Must reflect quantifiable outcomes, excluding general "feel good"/ generic statements like "we intend to take a leadership position blah blah blah."
3. This includes justifying the process itself whereby financial assumptions, market statistics, trends and forecasts need to be sourced and footnoted. Anything less will challenge the credibility of the Plan.

4. Financial forecasts need to reflect the best guestimates of the writer(s). Exaggerated revenue streams and profits will be scrutinized and questioned. Again, all assumptions require explanations as to how they were assembled.
5. Goals can be haughty, but not ridiculously so as to question their believability.
6. If the Plan reflects an opportunity or growth strategy that is time sensitive with a limited window, it should be stated. Two such examples are when new competitors or technology are coming on stream and your company is obligated to act to meet the challenge.
7. Finally, the Business Plan needs to be eminently readable. That means less "ivory tower" and more charts, graphics, photos, and a user-friendly layout. Formatting seems like a minor issue, but it is not. If the reader gets bored before reaching the crux of the Plan, it becomes a useless effort.

Business Plan Mistakes and Their Impact

That having been said, here are the most common Business Plan mistakes. See if you recognize any of these shortcomings in your own existing or "work in progress" Business Plan.

- It is an error assuming that the outside/third-party reader knows your company and your marketplace. Far too often Business Plans are written with little background or company insight which are critical in order for the reader to appreciate your Plan, who you are, and where your goals and strategies originate from.
- Goals are admirable. However, goals without a strategy or pathway to realizing those goals is called "wishful/pie in the sky thinking." The Plan becomes a story without a plot.
- Plans written by the enthusiastic entrepreneur often tend to wander to and fro, covering a wide and sometimes unrelated swath. Focus is important.
- Plans based on catch-up, namely working hard after falling well behind, as opposed to being closer to the forefront of change,

reduce the merit of the Plan's strategies. Catch-up is not a good starting point as it smacks of desperation.

- Market research that is insufficient, outdated, or skewed to whatever data you WANT to believe is ALWAYS a Plan killer.
- Competition that you do not consider a threat will likely outlive you. Pay attention.
- A well-defined Value Proposition is critical. Are you meeting identified marketplace needs, as further justified by research and support/properly sourced data?
- Risk is often quashed by enthusiasm. A true Business Plan treats risk with the respect it deserves.
- The Business Model chosen for your enterprise needs to clearly deliver monetization, highest margins, and best identified market. Anything less will be questioned.
- Overly lengthy Business Plans rarely get read cover to cover by outside parties. Important information entombed within a voluminous Plan often stays buried.
- Finally, your Plan should justify your ability to take on the challenge. You and your team should have the credentials and experience to spearhead the pathway toward the end deliverables.

If your Business Plan adheres to the rules in this chapter that exemplify a successful Business Plan, and remains cognizant of, and avoids a Plan's potential flaws, your chances of fulfilling your intended strategies are greatly improved. A well-conceived Business Plan is your capital.

A Business Plan that achieves in delivering the results it sets out to secure is the ultimate test of the entrepreneurs' ability to touch their audience. Their intended readership. That also includes providing you with a business roadmap to pursue.

The Global World Web (GWW) goal was to establish a business-to-business (B2B) model web to run parallel to the existing internet, but limited to a corporate client base, and without any personal web content that was flooding and slowing down conventional internet avenues.

While being ambitious, it presented viable data justifying the apparent need for GWW. Also, it had garnered cautious interest from a handful of communications companies.

GWW's self-inflicted mistakes, however, were gargantuan.

- The optimistic revenue projections were in hundreds of billions, commencing within four to six months of GWW's launch, a prediction that defied logic.
- The GWW Plan listed committed prominent partners among telco communications companies, but, in reality, these companies had limited their position as "interested observers" only.
- The assumptions for the financial statements consumed 47 pages. Scrutiny was painful.
- The Business Plan itself was well over three hundred pages, thereby, again, almost guaranteeing readers would carry out a cursory review at best.
- The risk factors were only marginally addressed. The founders believed the risks were minimal. They were actually mammoth.
- Most damaging of all was the "ask" of five hundred million start-up dollars for which the founder was offering ten percent ownership. And that was described as "first tranche funding" only.

The concept shifted from interesting to highly unrealistic by virtue of a Business Plan that was disastrously optimistic and unsupportable on numerous levels. GWW failed to leave the launchpad, to nobody's great surprise.

Score	Good Mistake Rating	Bad Mistake Rating	Ugly Mistake Rating
3			
2			
1			

Lesson(s) Learned: GWW's shortsightedness and steadfast adherence to unrealistic expectations hollowed out the venture's ability to leave the starting gate. The concept was reasonably innovative, but that's where it ended. GWW's Business Plan presented overestimated revenues, short-term success expectations, and huge investment needs that did not even recognize risks. GWW offered only a ten percent stockholding to the money players and that too led to GWW's demise. The project itself was fixable, and could have been salvaged with a serious rethink, but the inflexibility of the founders to address GWW's inherent weaknesses as packaged into a dreamscape Business Plan, gave GWW an aura of a pipedream.

The case study earned a "3" in the "Bad Mistake Rating" chart, mainly because all the major concerns and flaws could have been dealt with had the founder not be blinded by his own Napoleonic stubborn beliefs of invincibility. The initiative was clever and likely salvageable, but the mindset of the founder was not.

CHAPTER 19

Budgeting Errors and Fixes

"A budget is telling your money where to go instead of wondering where it went."

—Dave Ramsey

A budget, in its simplest definition, is a financial roadmap of expectations: revenues, gross margins, labor, expenses, profits, and cash flow. In practice, it has two real-world applications.

- A vehicle to control costs and assure adherence to a model designed to deliver financial returns, and
- the ability to compare your actual performance against the budgetary predictions in order to identify gaps, revenue shortfalls, cost overruns, decreasing margins and profits, and greater demands on your cash flow, and take timely remedial action.

The design and preparation of a budget is a combination of best guesstimating, using hard data where available, wishful thinking, and the art of conjuring. Taken together, a budget can be a powerful monitoring and strategic planning tool for a business. However, the compilation of a budget lends itself to a number of potential mistakes.

Budget Mistakes

- Over or underestimating revenues and costs, the result of which directly biases the bottom-line predictions
- Use of estimates even where historical hard data is available, to be used as a foundation for budget line items
- Inaccurate cash flow scenarios, mostly because that is what you want to happen and not what is likely to happen. The result can often be a real cash crunch that leaves you unprepared.

- Casting a budget as a one-time, static document instead of a living, breathing, ever-changing guide that needs to be revisited and possibly updated regularly. An outdated budget is of little use.
- Setting unachievable targets that lead to a budget being set aside
- Maintaining budget secrecy in a business, instead of sharing all or parts with managers, all of whom can also be encouraged to input their suggestions and feedback.

Budget "Red Flag" Mistakes Can Be Converted to Benefits

The following are often considered as cautionary "red flags" in budgeting, but should also be recognized as pathways to positive outcomes of the forecasting predictive process.

- Monitor cash and cash flow. Cash is your business's lifeblood.
- Proper debt management implies spending only at an affordable rate for highest priority expenditures and capital assets.
- Differentiate between "needs" and "wants."
- If and when your profits decline, or any one expenditure skyrockets, every red flag in sight should start waving for attention. Find the source of the leakage.
- Constantly missing budgeted revenue projections is disheartening. Either be more realistic about your sales expectations or identify and fix the weak links that are driving down income.
- Everyone wants growth, but be pragmatic with your ambitious progress predictions.
- Gut feelings are not adequate predictors. Wherever and whenever possible, base your budget on historical data and trends and applying adjusted future expectations.
- There are certain market and economic factors that are beyond your control, such as inflation, trade wars/tariffs, or economic downturns. While you cannot predict the impact of these outside stress factors, you can provide provisions for these impacting in your budget. Remain vigilant about the unexpected and the "miscellaneous" which almost always surface.

- Build KPIs into your budget as an added feature to monitor trends, and to identify possible problematic issues before or as they arise.
- Try to create a budget that is balanced. If it is too restrictive/conservative, it can choke performance. Conversely, if it is openly generous, then it can promote relaxed spending that may be detrimental.
- Practice flexibility in planning and provisioning.
- Update your budget quarterly to reflect the realities of market changes and economic shifts.
- Use the budget for regular, timely comparisons with actual performance. Your budget has value that can help you run your business.

One of my contracts was to review and provide due diligence on investment opportunities for a venture fund. As an outsider, with no inherent connections with the candidates, I was in an ideal situation to provide unfettered input.

One proponent offered an interesting and innovative medical technology that, frankly, had me second-guessing myself. I was caught between enthusiasm and serious questioning. The following were my key findings.

- The technology was still only partially developed with no "proof of concept" yet available.
- Revenue projections were enough to make readers salivate, but, in reality, there was zero track record of market uptake.
- Marketing and introductory promotional expenses, which one would expect to be astronomical for new health care technology, were very conservative. When questioned, the founders assumed instant market acceptance. I took this to be wishful thinking. There were very few potential user Letters of Interest or scientific media published introductory articles.
- Company management stood by their budget, including opinions cited by their CFO. Flexibility and openness were not demonstrated.

My recommendation was to reject the investment request, but to also purchase a "First Right of Refusal" as a safeguard, which my investor client did.

Score	Good Mistake Rating	Bad Mistake Rating	Ugly Mistake Rating
3			
2			
1			

Lesson(s) Learned: Well prepared budgets are often reader oriented. Done for your own company, budgets tend to be more conservative, and rightly so. However, in other situations, as was the case in this example, the proponent delivered an over-the-top budget and, incidentally, an equally scintillating Business Plan which made reading interesting, but more so from a dreamscape vantage point. The company, unable to raise investment, sold the business to a multinational and my client sold their First Rights in the transaction, at an impressive profit. They actually sent me a thank you note for my timely advice. My contingency fees were my real reward.

A business idea or proposal, regardless of how potentially exciting it might be, but built on fluff, is difficult to rate. In this instance, the mistake was serious because if the goal was to attract investment capital, it failed by delivering nothing tangible or justifiable. Had more effort been directed toward convincing the reader(s) as to the projects merit, it might have lived on to succeed. Instead, it deflated in on itself, earning a "2" in the "Bad Mistake Rating."

CHAPTER 20

Funding Request Mistakes Are Avoidable

"Some debts are fun when you are acquiring them, but none are fun when you set about retiring them."

—Ogden Nash

The number one cause of failure of a business is a lack of cash. A cash crunch is a stick thrust into the spokes of progress.

One of the top fears of businesspeople is asking for money.

Funders/Investors and borrowers: Strange bedfellows.

Yet quite often the mistakes entrepreneurs make in preparing to approach a funder or investor seem to defy common sense. **Each of these mistakes below virtually guarantees rejection**.

- An incomplete or poorly thought-out Business Plan, that has gaps that a funder can drive a truck through, is a certain deal killer. Shortcomings and errors might include no justified Value Proposition, that is, no proven need for a product or service, or a budget and funding "ask" that do not meet the needs of the venture.[7] Those are only two of many of the "funding don'ts."
  Key funding roadblocks are listed below:-
  - Believing that your company's risk factor is marginal and conveying simplistic optimism to the funder.
  - Requesting funds for frivolous items defined as any expenditure or capital item not directly delivering value and revenues for the business.

---

[7]This book contains a chapter "Business Plan Mistakes" that can help the reader avoid these and other presentation issues.

- Presenting outdated or incomplete market research. This is an item that garners instant negative attention from the funder/investor.
- Delivering an elevator pitch that is not inspiring.
- Assuming the funding party knows the intricacies of your company. That is rarely the case. It is prudent to present as if you are speaking to a first grader.
- Presuming the banker is your friend. That is not the case (even at Christmas). They have a role to play and that is protecting the depositors' money and the banks' profits. Understand that and govern yourself accordingly at the meetings.
- Understating your capital requirements and assuming you can return shortly to request a second funding tranche. This might not be the case.
- Relying on historical financial statements that have little relevance to your financial conditions today.
- Even a lack of confidence in your style and body language can sway a funder or investor.
- Evidence of a high burn rate or a high-level break-even analysis. These are red flags for any investment or funding source.
- Assuming your personal credit worthiness does not impact your corporate funding requests. It does. That includes your availability of collateral and security to offer funders and investors.
- Reimbursement of past loans. Your history of meeting your previous debt obligations is a determining factor from a lenders' perspective.

Learning from Funding Mistakes

- Be very cognizant of, and ready to speak to exactly what you are asking for, why you are seeking the funds, what you will use the funds for, and what the injection will do for your business.
- Review all the "funding don'ts" listed in the previous section of this chapter and assure that you have taken note of the conditions

that can diminish your chances of securing the funding you are requesting.

- Practice your elevator pitch before any meetings. Also, it may be worthwhile to role play any upcoming funder meetings with a mentor who can provide insight and recommendations and identify potential problematic pitch areas.
- Loans and investments are deal transactions. Feel free to partake in the discussions by asking questions and suggesting terms such as repayment plans that are better for your business. Focus on more than simply loan rates. Be a participant.
- Work to build a professional relationship with the funder and not a close personal one. Keep them separate.
- It is viable to approach more than one funding source. A "Plan B" is always a good idea. In some instances, a second funder can provide impetus for the primary source you have initially approached to act. Leverage often works.
- Research the funders' website and published criteria to understand how your needs fit into their priorities, and how your business sector is perceived by their funding team.
- Maintain solid financial records that may be called upon to be produced during the course of the discussions.
- As a final, but hugely important item, be very cognizant of whom you are asking for money. Most lenders follow industrywide lending standards, but there are always a few who have quick "trigger fingers" in recalling loans. Ask around.

There is also a category of investors referred to as "vulture capitalists." While most investor funds naturally focus on PPE priorities (**p**rofit, **p**rotection or security, and a well-defined **e**xit **s**trategy), there are other funds that can hamstring your business. They do so by demanding that you meet certain milestones, generally revenue levels and profits, and if you fail to do so, they would be entitled to penalties. These generally represent you forfeiting a percentage of your shares for every milestone missed, or steep fines or renegotiated investment terms. Run away from these vulture funders.

The company was the largest shellfish aquaculture harvester and processor on the west coast of North America with processing and international shipping facilities scattered throughout the United States and Canada.

The industry was highly competitive, and, as new shoreline (foreshore) licensing territories opened up, a feeding frenzy broke out among the stakeholders. These new opportunities were extremely expensive and competitive.

Our client was anxious to bid, but caught between seasons, cash flow was limited. We were hired to attract new capital. Included in the terms and conditions of our contract, we insisted on two clauses: (1) the creation of a funding attraction package/new Business Plan which we were to undertake, and (2) that the client also works to find funders. We felt that a two-pronged approach that sought alternate sources of funding, Plan A and Plan B, was a viable approach. This was also in consideration of the clients' desire to close the financing "yesterday." The opportunity window was short-lived.

We launched our search among traditional lenders as well as our network of investment funders.

The client chose a different route, negotiating with some money players we were not very familiar with, but their reputation tweaked some red flags.

Coincidentally, both we and the client secured proposals almost simultaneously. Ours represented more expensive money, but with easier terms, while the clients' secured offer had a lower interest but what we defined as "vulture investor" terms.

The client chose the source they had identified, mostly because the closing date was better. While we could not dissuade them, and warned them vociferously about the penalty clauses, they remained oblivious to the dangers.

We did, however, manage to persuade them to accept one of our strategies, and that was to protect all their valuable holdings in a new shell company, as an additional firewall, and carve off only the asset being funded into a Newco. They heeded our advice.

Within one year, with penalties added up, thanks to unachievable targets, the vulture fund held 57 percent of the operating business Newco, an increase from 48 percent which they had originally held. Further, decision making for our client became a matter of following the wishes of the principal shareholder.

Our client divested themselves of their Newco shares, breathed a sigh of relief, thanked us most generously for our forewarning strategy, and became our loyal customers.

Score	Good Mistake Rating	Bad Mistake Rating	Ugly Mistake Rating
3			
2			
1			

Lesson(s) Learned: Decision making is a thoughtful process where all aspects require close examination. There are always those who play by their own rules and careful deliberation is a requirement. The age-old adage is that if something looks too good, it generally means trouble ahead. And when in doubt, try building in escape clauses that will help extricate you from potential distress.

Greed is often fatal, and sometimes presents itself as the easiest way out of a problem or mistake. This may not be the most efficacious strategy. In this instance, the company walked blindly into a vulture capital quicksand pit from which there was no escape. A catastrophic decision cost them the company. A "3" on the "Ugly Mistake Rating" was well deserved.

CHAPTER 21

Market Research Snafus and Getting Meaningful Results

"Whatever failures I have known, whatever errors I have committed, whatever follies I have witnessed ... have been the consequences of action without thought."

—Bernard Baruch

Almost every conceivable aspect of your company, who you are, what you do, how you package yourself and your product service, and how you strategize your growth, all are grounded in market research.

Every business decision should be driven by timely and meaningful market research that provides the answers to the questions you should ask. From positioning your business in the marketplace to identifying the expertise and experience of the people you hire and the team you build, market research provides the company's foundation and direction.

Your business marketplace is analogous to pie. You and a host of competitors vie for choice slices of the pie, and your effectiveness is determined by your market penetration strategies, which, in turn, are driven by implementing the actionable deliverables of the market research you carry out.

Everything is interconnected. Mistakes can be costly, well beyond any financial impact.

Market Research Core Deliverables	Market Research Is Your Capital
Answers key questions: who will buy from you? Why would they choose you? Are your prices on target? Are your distribution channels working? Is your target market and customer base best suited for your business?	Justification that your business will succeed, or is on the right trajectory, or, conversely, that you need to take action to protect or re-energize your marketing approach

Market Research Core Deliverables	Market Research Is Your Capital
Facilitates learning about yourself and/or your competitors	Product need—assesses the merits of your Value Proposition
Uncovers gaps and weaknesses before they harm your operations. Recommends corrective action.	Identifies potential role models to follow
	Instills confidence in your ability to perform
Reaffirms the effectiveness of your brand	Slows your decision-making process which, as an entrepreneur, can often be dangerously "knee jerk"
Identifies new target market niches previously not considered	
Forewarns changing marketplace trends	Confirms (or rejects) the viability of the Business Model you have chosen
	Facilitates your long-term planning process

Market Research Mistakes

- Neglecting, bypassing or giving little credence to market research is a fundamental error and risk.
- Underestimating the demands on your business by leaping into decisions that are not based on hard facts or competition and trends uncovered during the market research process.
- Cherry picking research to select only the market research results you want to believe.
- Undervaluing or overvaluing product or service market access points can be fatal or require costly corrective backtracking on price or distribution/market penetration.
- Ignoring customer feedback. Disregarding input from your primary source of revenues. Surveys, customer satisfaction polls, and other input mechanisms yield vital suggestions to act upon, or problems to deal with. Carry them out regularly and don't disregard the results.
- Taking customers for granted instead of celebrating their loyalty and showing your appreciation.
- Assuming you are as good or better than your competition, and doing so without any supporting proof. This arrogance can be disastrous.

- Business ego-bluster is off-putting to customers as well.
- Going after a broader market than you are capable of servicing severely limits your very ability to serve your current markets. Market research will identify your prime target market and customer base.
- Ignored market research often breeds complacency, which is not an endearing feature. Business or market share losses almost always follow. Competitors leapfrog over you or capture part of your market share that you may have lost or watched as it slipped away.
- A simple act of asking the wrong or misleading questions in your market research undertaking can yield erroneous or incomplete results. Be precise.

Correcting Market Research Mistakes or Shortcomings

- Field research. Visit competitors. Speak to potential customers and ask where else they do business.
- Do long-distance research with similar businesses but located outside your region. They will often provide valuable insight.
- Access trade magazines and newsletters and reports issued by organizations catering to you and your competitors.
- Join in networking events, including conferences, trade shows, and exhibitions.
- Form material alliances with noncompeting stakeholders who also serve your industry and your customer base.
- Carry out surveys, garner customer satisfaction input.
- Constantly revisit your Value Proposition. Monitor changes in marketplace and user needs.
- Keep asking yourself who your customers are and how to best influence and serve them.
- Don't hurry or short-change the research process.
- Search for commonality of information or responses in the data gathered.
- Believe market research data. Don't prejudge the results.
- When you identify mistakes you might be making, learn from them, and take corrective action. Learning is your capital.

- **Very importantly, use market research.** Don't just gather data. Involve market research into every facet of your business and in your decision-making process.

Our client was faced with a formative problem. They had developed a highly innovative consumer shopping program which offered an enlightened grocery store experience for shoppers.

The technology was complex, but the user interface was clean and simple. From a development aspect, the product was a winner.

When shoppers entered the store carrying their store rewards card, their name would crop up on a huge LED screen, and might read something like,

> Mrs. Smith, last week you bought 2% milk at $3.75 a quart. Today, it's on sale for $2.25 in aisle 3. While there, have a look at the assortment of ice cream on sale. Your family might enjoy the chocolate ripple ice cream you bought three weeks ago. Happy shopping!

It was Orwellian. Big brother personified.

The problem was that, on the several beta tests carried out as a prerequisite to grocery chains signing on, the uptake was marginal at best. Invasive and hostile at worst. Even gifts and generous coupons did little to persuade prospective users to adopt the technology. The shopping public reaction was abysmal, and, subsequently, the major grocery chains were leery to become clients.

The root cause of this dilemma was simple—nobody really asked the customers. The software company simply assumed everybody would benefit and adopt this technology. They convinced themselves.

A review of their so-called market research demonstrated how subjective their data was. A typical question was "How much do you like this service as a guide to your shopping experience? 1 for very much, 2 for quite a lot, 3 for interesting." There was no open-ended comments area, and no negative input choices.

When we conducted a new in-person survey which was much more fruitful, we discovered that shoppers felt this service was highly intrusive. They detested being singled out on a huge screen and have their likes and dislikes shared with the public.

The resolution we recommended was creative. Rather than using a highly visible screen, simply attach small screens onto the shopping carts, in plain sight of the shopper only and broadcast personalized written-only messages to each of the shoppers.

It worked. Uptake increased dramatically, and several grocery chains agreed to launch into the next beta stage, that being installing the service at several test store locations.

Meaningful market research prevailed.

Score	Good Mistake Rating	Bad Mistake Rating	Ugly Mistake Rating
3			
2			
1			

Lesson(s) Learned: Carry out impartial market research and repeat the process quarterly. Most importantly, heed the results and make sure that your approach reflects the needs and wishes of your customers. You supply. They buy. The relationship is symbiotic.

The company, faced with a setback, pivoted quickly enough to carry on with successfully implementing a modified version of its shopping concept. A "2" on the "Good Mistake Ratings" was earned.

CHAPTER 22

Creating a Marketing Plan That Almost Defies Mistakes

> *"Be yourself and think for yourself, and while your conclusions may not be infallible, they will be nearer right than the inclusions forced upon you by those who have a personal interest in keeping you in ignorance."*
>
> —Elbert Hubbard

You have scads of well-defined market research that is pointing you toward reaching a marketplace that is anticipating and welcoming your products or services. All that remains is an actionable and realizable Marketing Plan as to how you will deliver what you promise.

Components of an Effective Market Plan

Meet or exceed your commitments by overdelivering on the key aspects of marketing: customer service, quality, price, and performance. Design a strategy on how you and all your people will do just that while effectively promoting/marketing yourself in the process. Here's how.

- Your company has a number of strengths, both externally influenced (customers, market, reputation, respect) and internally (team attitude, customer service, well-received products/services). Build on those strengths. They are your capital.
- Make yourself memorable and recognizable.
- Markets change, often unexpectedly, or even minutely, just enough to throw you off your game plan. Stay diligent to market conditions, and their ebb and flow.

- Your competitors are likely monitoring everything you do. Stay in close touch with what they are doing, including new policies, new (or terminating) products or services, promotional strategies, and other shifts that will reflect on your own marketing and general operational activities.
- Establish a system to quantify the results of your marketing, and any increases or decreases attributable to them over time. Take any action required to maintain your market foothold.
- Is your customer profile changing? Newcomers? Different demographics? Monitor and assure you are serving the needs of the CURRENT market. Define and live by your Value Proposition, i.e., a proven need for what you do or sell.

Market Plan Mistakes

- Bad market research guarantees a poor Marketing Plan.
- Setting unattainable performance standards will frustrate your team as they may view their assigned deliverables impossible to reach, followed by "why bother trying." Failing to set quantifiable goals will blur the purpose of your Marketing Strategy.
- Your Value Proposition is a key yardstick, yet many companies sell what they themselves want to, or what they feel the market needs without verifying if that is actually the case.
- Copycat Marketing Plans, those closely replicating competition, are often perceived by customers as second rate, or imply you cannot be bothered to try for a degree of originality.
- Upon close examination you will find that you can compile a customer profile for whom you can develop attraction strategies. Failing that, your target buying audience is often too large to serve adequately.
- Understanding what drives a customer, what are their "hot buttons" insofar as doing business with you, is critical. Ask them. Document their responses. If you circumvent the results, or your Marketing Plan is vague, you will miss the target.
- An integral component of a Marketing Plan is to generate a budget and define how and where the funding will be spent. Far

too many company marketing budgets are "hit and miss," or underfunded, likely because the Marketing Plan does not properly address budget allocation.

Simple Steps to Create a Workable and Implementable Marketing Plan

1. You need a starting point. What do you want to achieve and in what timeframe?
2. Quantify your expectations. Set milestones.
3. Define your market strategy in terms of your mainstay products/services, where customers will find out about you what promotional vehicles are most effective for delivering your message into the marketplace, including SEO (Search Engine Optimization) content creation.
4. Carry out focus groups or surveys to gauge the effectiveness of your brand and what triggers people to think of you or remember you. These are the hot buttons you will need to use in your campaigns.
5. Allocate a sufficient budget to carry out your Marketing Plan activities.
6. Create an Action Plan to deliver your plan and assign specific tasks to your team.
7. Tracking is critical. Is your Marketing Plan working? Build a package to track results using whatever metric is appropriate for your sector.
8. Review the results quarterly, or faster, and do not hesitate to alter your plan in accordance with changing times, shifting demographics, technology, new or more aggressive competition, and morphing market needs and expectations (Value Proposition).

SWARM was a pet project of mine. The seed was planted during my years of doing business in China.

Consumers, weary of escalating prices, formed bargaining groups. Potential buyers, all after a similar product such as appliance, car or renting an apartment, would band together and approach a vendor or supplier and demand discounts for all parties in the group.

In some instances, a SWARM could compromise a hundred or more buyers, which represented a substantial transaction for the seller. The SWARM carried a significant buying clout, and the concept grew dramatically.

Why not bring SWARM to North America? That was my thought. I assigned the market research to an associate.

He reported back to me within two months with a preliminary research report that conditionally endorsed the concept and even included a Marketing Plan for its launch.

While I was generally pleased with the results, I questioned the glowing positivity of the results. I had one last nagging question to pose for the Marketing Plan author.

"This is a Chinese initiative with a strong cultural sway. Will the North American consumer react with the same zeal as the Chinese public? Run some focus groups to gauge people's reaction to SWARM's need for organized, large public buying group action."

The response was negative. North Americans were interested in product brands, technology, serviceability, warranties, and availability. Price was not always the uppermost consideration.

SWARM never launched and a Marketing Plan based on a flawed strategy was buried with it. The market researcher who only reported what he assumed I had hoped to hear was dismissed.

Score	Good Mistake Rating	Bad Mistake Rating	Ugly Mistake Rating
3			
2			
1			

Lesson(s) Learned: A Marketing Plan that reflects impartial market research, a well-defined market strategy, and a Value Proposition that justifies filling a real need in the marketplace are all intertwined. They depend on each other. Any one element missing, faltering or representing a weak link is fatal. That was the case with SWARM. The best authored Marketing Plan for such an iffy opportunity is not a salvation. Interesting idea, but time to move on.

We did not consider all elements that would have impacted the venture, from cultural differences and consumer buying habits to competition from sellers well-entrenched in the marketplace. A "2" "Bad Mistake Rating" is justified. The implications of the oversights were serious and helped shelf the idea. Perhaps a change in the operational game plan adapting SWARM to the North American market could have saved the initiative.

CHAPTER 23

Launch Mistakes; Righting the Wrongs

"The way to get started is to quit talking and begin doing."

—Walt Disney

Fatal or near fatal mistakes are commonplace in the start-up phase, or for an established business launching a new product or service. Too common. And they may encompass virtually every facet of a business, starting with assumptions made in the prelaunch phase. These represent only a handful of blunders that can impact your ability to succeed.

Prelaunch Mistakes

- A Value Proposition that is geared toward the founders' own concept as opposed to the identified needs of the marketplace, and the customer base. Promoting and selling what you want versus what the buyers actually need is a certain nonstarter.
- Insufficient or incomplete market research in conjunction with believing only what market research results you want to, and intentionally ignoring red flags. This can include not paying attention to invaluable customer feedback that really should be guiding your decision making.
- Poor execution. Where there is a gap between planning and implementation, the results can be disastrous.
- This mistake comes up repeatedly, namely, a poor Business Plan with an overly aggressive launch Action Plan both in expectations and timelines.

Funding

- Securing sufficient funding, investment or capital. Little else can apply the brakes to a start-up or operating business faster than insufficient funds. The implication here is that budgeting may not have recognized pending shortfalls, or an owner assuming they can run on fumes.

Marketing

- Product or service pricing that works on a markup model that does not cover costs or has little wiggle room in the event of lower-than-expected margins or expense overruns.
- A newly developed brand that does little to garner interest and may not be memorable enough for clients to become repeat customers. Ineffective messaging is a lost opportunity.
- Little recognition that a comprehensive market penetration strategy and an achievable Marketing Plan are critical components of capturing market share.
- An ill-defined customer profile indicates a lack of understanding as to who should be buying from you, and therefore how you should be packaging yourself and your offerings to a desired customer base.

Competition

- Staying attuned to competition is a good strategy. However, jealousy of competitors can lead to irrational knee jerk/"let's play catch-up" marketing and operational decisions.

Resources

- Employing the right people can deliver results. Alternatively, selecting the wrong people becomes an impediment to the resources of the business. They slow you down.
- Hiring people late to fix a problem is not as sound as engaging the right people early enough to be responsible for avoiding hiccups.

- Leadership is also key but often lacking. Solid communications skills and the ability to motivate and selectively micromanage the team are all critical components of an effective leader. Leadership should be part of any launch strategy.
- Delegation and teamwork, especially during the launch phase, work far better than the founder/owner trying to, but not able to do everything.
- Building business friends and allies and networking before or as you launch are crucial. When things veer off course, business friends are there to help.
- IP is a significant asset but often sits unprotected and open to technology scavengers.

Timing

- Launching too early or too late can impact its effectiveness and deliver significantly lower results and returns. This applies equally to start-ups as well as established companies introducing new products or services to the marketplace

The preceding lists a number of warnings and "do nots" that represent mistakes during the launch phase of a company or during the introduction of products/service for an existing business. Some are fixable, others may be fatal. Most are somewhere in between.

The successful entrepreneur or manager remains diligent, monitors the consequential development of the business, learns from any real or perceived problems and reacts quickly. Not in a knee-jerk fashion, but in a timely manner to prevent damage. And, even more importantly, adds these lessons to a resource toolbox to deal with these challenges the next time they arise. And, in business, they likely will.

I was approached by a group looking to start an online business mentoring school. I was asked to teach, which I agreed to do once the school was up and running, and I was also invited to participate financially as an investor/partner. I declined, stating that I might consider once the school was in operation for over eight months and with a full complement of students.

My unease covered a host of red flags, most of which I shared with the founders.

- The name they chose, "The No B!S! Business School" ("NBBS") was, in their opinion, clever. There were several other schools with similar semi-offensive names, which they were modeling after. However, these other schools had programs that reflected their outrageous namesakes, while NBBS was to be more traditional. I felt the name and content offered were mismatched.
- Their pricing structure was complicated and muddled with various hard-to-follow options. Also, their business model included a subscription service, and a monetization format that was becoming increasingly unpopular.
- Market research would have indicated a crowded marketplace.
- Funding was barebones and inadequate to launch with any flair.

The school launched and ran for five months, with a marginal uptake. Its name and graphics package carried it at the onset, more out of curiosity than serious sign-up intent.

Score	Good Mistake Rating	Bad Mistake Rating	Ugly Mistake Rating
3			
2			
1			

Lesson(s) Learned: A business cannot fly by good intentions alone, or be readily ushered into existence, especially when there are a host of visible and reasonably fixable red flags. Launching a business or an established company introducing new products or services has an extensive toolbox of resources to help increase their chances of success.

This venture earned a "3" in the "Ugly Mistake Rating" mainly because the owners chose to launch a business for which there was no identified need or desire. The cost of a market awareness-building campaign would also have been prohibitive for the founders.

SECTION THREE

Operational Mistakes

Assume strategic planning is complete. Newcos have gone through their prelaunch preparation and working companies have girded themselves for the introduction of new products and services, or are simply preparing for any inevitable change that the marketplace, technology, or shifting economic conditions offer up.

Once a business is operational, a new series of challenges await.

Planning versus implementation is transformative. It is an opportunity to shine, or struggle, to put into play everything you have learned, including lessons from roadblocks and miscues encountered, or simply a continuation of doing things wrong and paying the price of obstinance.

The previous Section deals with forewarning. This section deals with performance.

We now offer up a more detailed analysis of challenges and potential mistakes categorized by key business activities, and offer solutions and lessons to be learned for the operational enterprise.

CHAPTER 24

Communications and Networking Mistakes: Hearing and Being Heard

Communication

"Saying hello doesn't have an ROI. It's about building relationships."
—Gary Vaynerchuck

Communication is the act of delivering a message. Spoken, body language, gesture, or by expression, all are forms of reaching out.

Communication is also the art of listening and learning and providing feedback/responses indicating that you have deciphered the message imparted on you.

What sounds simple and common sense is often like the children's game of "broken telephone." What is spoken is often misinterpreted or only partially picked up, and as the same message gets passed along the chain, the result is often further garbled and miscommunicated.

In business, the ability to communicate is vital. Such mistakes can be costly.

- Not listening or listening while otherwise distracted fails to deliver a legitimate response and can result in an unintended action or reaction.
- Messaging by email or any other electronic avenue does not guarantee that the communiqué was received in the spirit with which it was sent. Digital messaging, which is usually brief, rarely provides the same direct feedback to the messenger that face-to-face provides.

- "Active listening" is never assured. The same applies to focused attention of both parties. Errors ensue. The two-way connection needs to be "live."
- Communication implies that the party or parties being addressed have background knowledge regarding the content of the message, which, if it includes any instructions or direction, may well go astray. Message delivery and message content receipt may not be a straight line.
- Particularly in today's tech world, acronyms and jargon are commonplace and there is no guarantee that those receiving the message are familiar with the significance of communication, or the emotion or the importance of it. The process is open to error.
- Most people are not trained in communication and presentation skills. The styles of each party involved in communicating may be different enough to warrant miscues in message delivery versus message received. Work to establish compatibility.
- Nonverbal cues and mannerisms form an integral part of communication, yet body language, eye contact, restless gestures, and even the tone and speaking levels often go unnoticed. They should not be ignored by either party.

The rules for effective communication are simple enough, but too often go unheeded.

- Verbal communication needs to be clear and concise with a singular clear message being the best for packaging the content. Don't crowd the playing field.
- The listener should confirm and acknowledge to you that the information / message delivered has been received and understood.
- Both or all parties need to be receptive and not distracted or otherwise engaged.
- Observe your own and the other parties' body language, facial expressions, gestures, and other nonverbal cues. Someone looking at their watch or checking their phone messages are non-starter cues.

- It is also recommended that you and your people undertake some very basic theater training. This will instill greater receptivity in communicating or being addressed.

Networking

"You can make more friends in two months by becoming interested in other people than you can in two years by trying to get other people interested in you."

—Dale Carnegie

Networking is a refined skill and involves a great degree of subtlety and role playing. In business, networking yields contacts, leads, multipliers who can act as connectors or stepping stones to others who may be of value to you, or offer revenue-generating opportunities themselves.

Networking is a two-way street. Reciprocity is key. You need to give up as much as you hope to receive back. Networking mistakes are often instant and lingering. The price in procuring leads and business can be substantial, but invisible since leads, connections, and business would simply not materialize in a networking situation void of mutuality.

Yet the mistakes in the art of networking often boil down to common sense. Each of these lapses can be inordinately expensive. Lost opportunities generally are.

- Don't be afraid to sell but wait your turn to jump into the fray. Being overeager is not an acceptable or attractive feature in a networking scenario.
- Listen before you speak. In this way you can assess the interests of the other parties and ensure any contributions you make to the conversation will align with their interest.
- Practice your elevator pitch in advance. Its significance cannot be overstated. Look for an opportunity to deliver it, but at the right moment. Gage the other parties' receptiveness.
- Join into groups, preferably not a group of your friends or business associates. Wallflowers make poor networkers.

- Make yourself memorable in your speech, appearance, and involvement with others in the group.
- Participate but never monopolize the conversation. Don't be a "network hog."
- Networking within a group is usually led by one or two parties. They are the ones that merit most of your attention.
- Avoid topics such as gossip, sex, politics, and religion. They are conversational alienators. Everything else is fair game.
- Flattery works, but not obsequious genuflecting.
- Wherever you can, research the attendees and their companies beforehand. Knowledge denotes interest. Unfamiliarity signifies disinterest.

When I hired Mark as a salesperson, I was most impressed with his verbal skills. His style was infectious, as was his ability to entertain and maintain the interest of others while he readied himself to go in for the kill.

These skills did not translate well when I joined him in sales meetings and network situations (trade shows, conferences, meet and greet events). He was like a Chatty Cathy Doll.[8] Like the prattling doll, Mark rarely stopped talking long enough to draw a breath. This is not a flattering handle.

It took months to train and retrain Mark to learn to take a step back and listen attentively to what others were talking about and how to more gently enter the flow of the sales visit or the networking opportunity.

Once this behavior was mastered, he was able to apply his salesmanship in an effective and productive manner. Yet, I never quite trusted his total conversion since, from time to time, he fell back into his old ways, as if the string in the Chatty Cathy Doll was pulled mercilessly.[9]

---

[8]"Chatty Cathy" refers to an overly talkative person, originating from the Mattel talking doll introduced in 1959. When the doll's string was pulled, it would say a few prerecorded phrases, making it the first successful talking doll. Today, the term is used informally to describe someone who talks excessively." https://en.wikipedia.org/wiki/Chatty_Cathy.

[9]See footnote 7 above.

Score	Good Mistake Rating	Bad Mistake Rating	Ugly Mistake Rating
3			
2			
1			

Lesson(s) Learned: Communication and networking skills are vital in business, and they can also be taught, harnessed, and molded into valuable resources in any businessperson's toolbox.

They are also easily abused if not properly monitored, and that can lose you opportunities.

Mark's communications and sales style was reprogrammed to fit our style and expectations. The result was positive, and this scenario earned a "2" in the "Good Mistake Ratings." Damages were contained and dealt with creating marginal disruptions only. The outcome was positive.

CHAPTER 25

Marketing Mistakes and Getting It Right

"People do not buy goods and services.
They buy relations, stories, and magic."
—Seth Godin

Marketing is a strategy that has significant impact if it is done right, and severe implications if it misses its intended mark.

"The aim of marketing is to know and understand the customer so well, the product or service fits him and sells itself" (*Peter Drucker*).

Yet marketing is one building block that delivers lessons to be learned and strategies to be abided to more so than any other area of business. It is often an adventurous undertaking that encourages creativity, expends vast amounts of funding and energy, and stays with the company for a long time as an invaluable asset, or an injurious stigma.

It has power. It implies attitude.

We live in the most media savvy generation in history that rejects much of the hype of yesteryear marketing. Companies are no longer "selling," but "serving," a concept companies need to adopt.

An Effective Marketing Mix

These are the core building blocks of effective marketing. They are within the company's sphere of influence and control and represent the traditional key components of the marketing jigsaw puzzle. To optimize marketing's impact, it is critical to get them all working in synergy with each other.

1. **CUSTOMER-DRIVEN**. Customers place the orders, pay the bills, and reorder if you treat them properly and with some reverence.

Fill their needs, which may change over time, and you will develop a loyal following.

2. **PRODUCT MIX**. Make it abundantly clear as to what you are selling and make it easy for the buying audience to quickly and effectively grasp what products or services you are marketing.
3. **PRICE**. While price is not always the deciding factor in the buyers' eyes, it is a method by which you can be compared to competitors and trends. As such, it needs to be within a pricing framework, unless you have a unique offering. An example of this was Apple's iPod, a stand-alone product in its day. It **was** the marketplace.
4. **CONTROLLABLE MARKET**. The effective marketer seeks out the smallest, controllable marketplace. The concept of selling to everyone everywhere is reserved for those companies that have the resources to carry an extended geographic outreach effectively.
5. **PLACEMENT**. What avenues you intend to use to deliver your product or service influences the exposure and attention it deserves. This also represents rolling out a Business Model, i.e., business-to-business, business-to-consumer, online sales, etc.
6. **PROMOTION**. This integrates branding; delivering a message users can grasp onto and deciding what venues will be used to bring your message to the customers' attention. Considering that buyers often have short attention spans, the impact of promotion needs to be swift, memorable, consistent, and ongoing.
7. **CREATIVITY**. Tell a story worth telling and worthy of people talking to others about you.
8. **LIVE IT**. Everyone on your team, every day, every contact with customers' needs to reflect what you want others to remember about you.
9. **STAY IN TOUCH**. Communication generates comfort, which translates to sales. Customers like to hear from you, but not via a continuous stream of cheesy pop-up ads. Teach them something about who you are, personal stories, and gentle introductions to new offerings. That's called relationship building.
10. **IF YOU DARE, JOLT PEOPLES' BRAINS WITH GUERILLA MARKETING**. The use of unsubtle guerilla marketing is often employed in ways customers don't expect, but can be so offbeat,

overdone or outrageous that it can miss its mark and cause damage as much as yield benefits. Control your impulse to shock and stand out without offending any one buying group.[10]

a. **Buzz Marketing:** word of mouth, social media, social networks
b. **Stealth Marketing:** subtle background placements in TV shows and videos
c. **Ambient Marketing:** casual product logo such as an advertisement at a bus stop station, park bench or in the lobby of a building
d. **Ambush Marketing:** coattailling at high profile events or well-recognized locations
e. **Grassroots Marketing:** distributing paper flyers, handouts, doorknob ads, or windshield ads.

A classic guerilla marketing illustration is a sandwich board placed in front of a bar/restaurant that reads, "Eat here or we will both starve." Pointed, clever, and effective.

Marketing Mistakes and Shortfalls Abound. These are the Greatest Threats.

As a keystone activity, marketing offers a host of possibilities that represent mistakes to avoid and learn from. Each lesson learned and added to your knowledge base makes you stronger, better at your role, and a contributor who brings greater value to the business.

A marketing mistake is simple to define: it's an initiative that does not work. The question is why not?

These missteps are to be avoided to assure a viable marketing campaign.

- Not knowing your customer profile can be disastrous. If you don't who you are selling to, or what they need, how can you solve their problems or meet their wishes? You likely won't.
- Misdirecting marketing insofar as promoting something(s) you want to sell as opposed to what the customer wants to buy. Sales uptick will be abysmal and, worst of all, you may not know why. Take your blinders off.

[10]"Guerrilla marketing involves unconventional and creative strategies to reach a target audience and generate excitement for a brand, product, or service."—Adam Hayes

- Not focusing your attention on the 80 percent of your clients who are your core of loyal regulars and, instead, chasing the occasional customers who account for a fraction of your buying base.
- Avoiding customer feedback/surveys/satisfaction reports because you might fear the results. The feedback is invaluable to keep you on track or to get you back in sync with your customers.
- Your employees are generally very in tune with your buyers. Seek out their feedback instead of ignoring this valuable source of marketing direction.
- Committing insufficient funds or attention to your marketing. This is one area where lost sales, declining market share or vanishing customers will cost you more than the marketing expenses you may have skimped on.
- Markets change. Customer profiles change. Demographics shift. Trends appear and disappear. Not keeping pace and adjusting your marketing strategies can be fatal.
- Stale or outdated inventory items that linger in your product mix tells the customers that you do not change in harmony with the times. You date yourself as "old school" or out of touch, neither of which is a flattering marketplace image.
- Waiting to launch a "perfect pitch" can rob you of the opportunity of remaining visible. Don't wait indefinitely.

A well thought-out Marketing Plan will most certainly identify the strategies, opportunities, and options that are open to you.

Further, it will encompass what lessons you have taken away from past marketing initiatives that succeeded, "almost worked," or fell off the cliff. **Learning from your past efforts is the capital that experience lays at your feet.**

Marketing applies to more than just companies promoting their goods or services. It applies equally to organizations, communities, and special interest groups with a message to deliver to a target audience.

My consulting company was contracted to work with several smaller North American west coast communities who shared an interest to grow, diversify, and attract younger families. Their resident population was aging, and their demographics were stagnating.

I decided that there were three viewpoints and desires that needed to be explored, hoping there would be some consensus among the parties. I felt that this was a crucial exercise before designing any marketing concepts.

1. I interviewed the community leaders to identify what their priorities would be. These turned out to be attracting young professionals and outside investment. While there was commonality between the community leaders' priorities, there were also differences that needed to be considered and integrated into the proposed marketing.
2. There were a number of nonresidents who had inquired about the various townships as a possible new homestead. I interviewed these interested parties to determine what would attract them to the region. Those features were safety, opportunities, natural beauty, and, in some cases, an exit plan to leave the big cities.
3. As a last component of my research, I identified other regions representing handfuls of communities and used them as role models. What worked? What didn't? what were the deciding features of their marketing initiatives? How long did it take? How did they quantify results in a meaningful way? Was there support from the residents in the communities?

With that ammunition in hand, my team and I developed a memorable name, "InvestWest" (pseudonym). Easy to remember. Easy to recall. Attached to that was a brand identification visioning line, *"Live Here, Play Here, Thrive Here, Invest Here"* that was similar to other tag lines that had proven successful elsewhere in the recent past. It covered all the bases.

The campaign was funded well enough to create some breathtaking graphics, social media, and website promotional pages. Further, I recommended hiring an agent to field calls, visits, and general inquiries, always assuming that a live person represents a warmer reception that an email, text message or voice mail. That individual was also charged to represent InvestWest at trade shows and events.

The initiative as designed by my firm was adopted by all the communities. It ran for two years and was deemed a success, if for no other reason than several technology companies moved their offices there, upscale coffee shops and specialty restaurants were opened by newcomers to cater to the tastes and needs of new arrivals. A shared resource business center and incubator was opened, and the blend of new residents enhanced the aging demographics of the region.

Score	Good Mistake Rating	Bad Mistake Rating	Ugly Mistake Rating
3			
2			
1			

Lesson(s) Learned: Marketing demands input from the client(s), a focus on their aspirations and priorities, and, even more importantly, recognition of the marketing needs and desires of the target audience. In this case, all elements came together, and success closely followed.

Campaign and branding recommendations were accepted and implemented, and the program proved highly successful. There were few hiccups, all of which were handled. A top "3" good rating is appropriate.

CHAPTER 26

Making Branding Mistakes Work for You

"...(Marketing) is the importance of building a desirable brand and solving customer problems"

—Philip Kotler and Clayton Christensen

Your brand is a promise. It stands for who you are, and how you want people to think of you, and remember you when "you are not in the room." Branding is being and staying memorable.

Your brand can deliver customer loyalty, a cornerstone of your business, and repeat clients. Loyalty is created by asking yourself: *Who do I want to serve? How do I want and need them to feel when I am serving them? Am I succeeding in delivering what they need and want and thereby enriching their experience?*

While your logo is one component of branding, it is not the only part of your mojo. Your slogan/tagline, website, social media presence, keynote marketing, offline presence, and the effectiveness of personal contact between your customers and your trained employees are all critical components of your brand.

Your Brand Is Equity and Financial Capital in Your Business

A brand has financial worth. It is often part of your business valuation and, as a business asset, it is also salable. It can have significant monetary value.

A brand's value is calculable using its cost of implementation, quantifying the markets it supports or income it generates. All are acceptable valuation estimating techniques. This is referred to as "brand equity"; the financial value gained from name recognition in terms of added profitability it delivers to your bottom line.

Further, investors are influenced by a brand that creates both quantifiable and qualitative market share for a company and thereby is a consideration in their investment decision making.

A brand has weight. It can be a significant line item on your balance sheet and places a value on recognition and reputation. It is capital and needs to be respected and fiercely defended accordingly.

Essential Features of a Successful, Impactful Brand

- Effective brands arouse emotion. They are a feeling, keeping in mind that, in today's "me first" marketplace, **you are selling service as much as any product**.
- Punchy messaging is effective. "Just Do It" is far more impactful and memorable than "We serve all your sporting needs with quality and commitment."
- Successful brands are built around visual cues and attitude. The bygone days of promotions built solely on price create very short-lived and forgettable market opportunities.
- The brand development process starts with asking yourself what you want to be known for by the customer niche you want to attract AND maintain.
- A company's ability to deliver on what it promises and to do so in a timely manner are both part of a brand. That builds reliability and loyalty.

Branding Mistakes

- A generic, often superlative message (i.e., "we are the best," "service like no other") is counterproductive. They are annoying and meaningless. Annoyed buyers go elsewhere.
- Branding is a total package of visuals, colors, taglines, memorable graphics, logo, and delivery. It demands consistency to be effective.
- It is a target effort needed to reach into the hearts and wallets of a defined audience. It cannot please or appeal to everyone. Focus on YOUR identified base.
- Timing is crucial, often incomprehensively horrible. I am often reminded of when CNN's broadcast of a war ravaging in the

Middle East and the starvation of its populace was interrupted by McDonald's ads. Anyone hungry?

- Which message delivery avenue to use? Market research will identify the ones logged into by your target customer base. Wrong selections will represent wasted precious marketing budgets.
- Your brand, like so many other facets of your business, like Business Plans and Financial Forecasts, are alive. Times change. Markets shift. People's needs morph. Branding needs to follow likewise. Branding is not stagnant. How often have you seen a beautifully attired, coiffed housewife dancing around the kitchen wielding a new-fangled sponge mop? Far too often and too recently I would guess. Makes you want to rush out and buy one? Highly unlikely.

Our firm was approached by a fast-food franchise seeking to expand their limited Southern U.S. market. They were considering the west coast as a prospect, although that was based on the founders' gut feel as opposed to definitive market research.

Their protein was rabbit: bunny burgers, bunny-in-a-basket, bunny wings (?), bunny nuggets, and hop-a-long kids packs. Their mascot that emblazoned their logo looked like a smiling Peter Cottontail holding a knife and fork.

It didn't take long to ascertain that the bunny-hugging Westcoast was the wrong market. A market survey left California and Washington's Gen X, Y and Z (and every other Gen) interviewees gasping, although rural Oregon apparently was more open.

Our suggestions represented a study in offbeat branding innovation.

- We said no to the Westcoast. That was the easy part. The founder concurred, not having been terribly committed to his shaky wishful thinking.
- The company had a small foothold (or paw hold) in Texas, and, what with that state being a country unto itself, we recommended going whole hog (or whole bunny, sorry, cannot help the puns)

and setting up a flagship there to spearhead franchising opportunities. They did.

- We suggested they change their mascot. We created a ripped, smirking (not just smiling) rabbit called "Buck" and instead of holding a knife and fork he was tending to a barbeque.
- All their product names now started with "Buck's own …"

This major branding shift worked. It was more of a rebirth. Buck was a star. Revenues grew in their home region, and Texas embraced their newly branded fast-food restaurants.

What we thought were outrageous branding changes had hit their mark, and we were rewarded accordingly, although I never took advantage of my lifetime Bucks discount card.

Score	Good Mistake Rating	Bad Mistake Rating	Ugly Mistake Rating
3			
2			
1			

Lesson(s) Learned: Branding often demands creativity, reaching beyond the scope of the norm and touching a nerve with the prospective customer base. A narrow focus can often lead to overly narrow results. Branding demands stepping outside the norms and weighing the fringe alternatives. Just ask Buck.

The branding rebirth and introduction of a new family of products were well received by the public. Owners were open to change and recognized the need to adapt, which they did. A Good Mistake rating of '3' was earned. (Regardless, one still can't help but feel sorry for those fluffy bunnies, right?)

CHAPTER 27

E-Commerce, Online, and Social Media Mistakes

"Success is stumbling from failure to failure with no loss of enthusiasm."
—Winston Churchill

The digital world is a universe of its own and worthy of an entire training and orientation program.[11] In this chapter we will mostly touch on how mistakes happen within these realms and how learning from them improves your abilities as a businessperson and adds capital both for yourself and your company.

Optimizing Your Presence

- Different digital platforms cater to specific sectors, whether it be online sales, special interest groups, mentoring, tech aficionados, fashion, charitable causes, exchange of ideas, meeting people (or soulmates), and other activity-specific objectives. Choose your venues carefully. Each will take time to build and thrive in, so a proper venue is hypercritical. Focus is key.
- The business model you choose to follow will affect your choice of venue and how you represent yourself and your business on the platform.
- The mechanics of order placement, shipping, joining, signing up for newsletters, and course/program registration need to be clear, concise and simple to access. Many are simply off-putting.

---

[11]Visit https://www.businessexpertpress.com/product-category/digital-social-media-marketing-and-advertising/, for a wide ranging library of digital, social media and marketing handbooks.

- Going online for whatever purpose is just the beginning. You must be discovered and stay relevant. That implies carefully selected keywords, SEO and placement. Ongoing vigilance and always being updated is keynote so that you move up the hierarchy of becoming found and remaining visible.
- For e-commerce, there are a host of avenues, from Etsy and Shopify to Amazon and Pinterest, among other lesser platforms. Try to employ the same content for several channels as a time-saving strategy and ease of updating these vehicles.

Errors Can Abound

- Overloading graphics and promotional pieces will slow visitors down when accessing your online site. Considering that people's marginal attention span ranges from two to eight seconds, and any slowdowns or delays they experience will move visitors along to your competitors at a click of the mouse.
- A landing page needs to be an attention grabber and not a fuzzy welcome mat. I don't want to know about your diplomas from the University of New Mexico or Tijuana. Tell me what you can do for me and how you might fulfill my needs.
- How do you know what I am after? That's where market research and profiling your intended customer base comes into play. Inadequate preparatory market research is a distinct error.
- Don't rely on a single channel to present yourself. People surf and you must also.
- Every venue offers limitless visitors' data and activity reports. Often far too much to be useful, but there are segments of these reports and input that you need to pay attention to. Ignoring feedback is a mistake.
- Visit competitor websites and online presence platforms, remembering that the world is your competition, not just the operation in your neighborhood. Span out. Find out what makes them work and how you can do or be better. Being a digital "also ran" is a formula for complacency.

PurAir (pseudonym) had assembled an air-purification/scrubber that claimed to destroy both viruses and bacteria. Invented by scientists, this unit was a ginormous beast suitable for large installations such as airplanes, hospitals, cruise ships, and commercial installations. Each sale proved to be a major task. Costs and skepticism were two principal roadblocks.

We were approached to research and brainstorm other markets that would benefit from this technology.

Firstly, we adopted the vantage point of a user. "Show me it worked" which they did, but it took sophisticated air monitoring/measuring technology to do so.

We posed three questions.

1. Can this equipment be downsized for consumer use? Viruses, bacteria, and pollution were serious considerations, particularly in crowded environments like offices, hospitals, care homes, and condominiums and houses. Places like China and India would be prime markets. The response was yes.
2. Can you develop a "magic stick indicator" that could demonstrate to the user that, when the color changed, undesirable air pollutants were being eliminated or absorbed, much like a pH stick. Again, the response was yes.
3. How could this be delivered to the marketplace and compete against the well-entrenched air purifiers that used HEPA (high efficiency particulate air) filters and the like? That was our responsibility.
   a. Market research identified the competitors and their mostly rudimentary technology. PurAir was light years ahead.
   b. The identified needs and health concerns of the marketplace were then built into a promotional campaign and marketing strategy that pressed the right hot buttons (fear, safety, health).
   c. We helped finalize the look of the consumer unit. The packaging needed to have a visual appeal.
   d. An outside production house was commissioned to supply the units, operating under a strict Nondisclosure Agreement.
   e. We identified online sales as the best venue, but this was a team of scientists we were dealing with. Marketing was beyond them, and managing a hired group of marketing professionals was foreign to them.

f. An online health product distributor was identified. They had credibility and an extensive network of customers, venues, and agents.
g. Chat sites were all established to encourage "word-of-mouth" promotion and to develop a loyal customer following. These were also the first customers who were approached with product updates and next model generation introductions.

We now had all the elements needed to bring PurAir to market and to be sold online. The larger commercial sales behemoths disappeared from PurAir's offerings, replaced by a successful consumer e-commerce campaign with the scientists sent scurrying back to the lab to develop PurAir V2. They were delighted.

Score	Good Mistake Rating	Bad Mistake Rating	Ugly Mistake Rating
3			
2			
1			

Lesson(s) Learned: In business everybody has their areas of expertise. There are very few capable business generalists. Particularly when it comes to e-commerce, online, and social media, there are those who thrive in this environment and they should be part of your team. Interestingly, the more I deal with these people, the more I realize how little I know about the magic they can deliver.

There were major pivots initiated by the company: meet the buyers' need to accept that the unit worked; generate an affordable consumer unit, and; institute direct online sales as a delivery mechanism. All changes once implemented spelled success for the company. A "3" in the "good ratings" column was well deserved.

CHAPTER 28

Operational/Day-to-Day Mistakes

"The most valuable thing you can make is a mistake—you can't learn anything from being perfect."

—Adam Osborne

In a business's daily life, there are four more categories worth briefly exploring from the assumption that mistakes are worthwhile learning tools. The lessons can certainly build your capital, the business's performance and your personal capabilities.

1. Tracking and accountability
2. Management style
3. Human resources
4. Governance

Tracking and Accountability

A business in full growth often lacks the interest to track expenditures, material or production costs, or even perform basic budgeting. The focus is on high-flying revenues and assuring adequate supply chains. However, the basic responsibilities of watching out for the best interests of the business may go by the wayside. And when the sales peaks flatten out or possibly even dwindle, as they tend to, or products reach their "best before" dates, the shortcomings of inadequate tracking and accountability rear up, red flags waving.

- Set specific milestones for your people
- Establish performance standards that are measurable

- Encourage each party's ownership of their areas of responsibility
- Track performance regularly, including in-person evaluations
- Expectations from all levels of management and staff need to be documented, measured, and reviewed regularly.
- Accountability needs to be consistent across the entire workforce of a business. Playing favorites breeds contempt and resentment.
- **Don't be complacent about success. Success can be temporary, or long term, but it is rarely forever. Reality awaits.** It can mean catching up with technology, or the need to pay attention to changing market trends and customer demands or acknowledging that change is imminent and calling out to you. Are you listening? Are you responding?

Management Style

- Effective managers learn to delegate while they simultaneously micromanage from afar.
- Poor managers, thinking nobody can do things as well as they can, tend to take on everything, usually well beyond their capacity and available time, and often exceeding their capabilities as well. The net result of this mistake is generally a distracted work environment, an insecure team unsure of their responsibilities, and the inept managers putting out fires they themselves have created.
- Planning and the implementation of the direction and goals set out in a Business Plan are key directives of management and considered a prime function. Effective management follows the game plan that can lead to opportunities. Managers who are lax in this regard tend to abide by the flavor of the day, which can be disastrous.
- Because managers often operate at the 20,000-foot level, they can better identify and manage risk. Its importance cannot be overemphasized.
- Also, keeping the personal and professional aspects separate helps maintain a structured management–employee relationship and makes it easier to call anyone on job performance, misjudgments or errors.

Human Resources

- Hiring, training, tracking performance, and empowering/delegating to employees are all critical components of human resources that are, well, human. Mistakes are often difficult to fix and can linger as the operation loses out on the value of employees.
- Overmanaging employees can be as detrimental as undermanaging.
- Similarly, onboarding or rushing new employs without sufficient orientation or training can create inconsistencies in the ebb and flow of an office environment.
- Further, an ineffective manager or owner who does not share their creative thoughts with those around them, or neglects to carry out or abide by existing strategic planning because "they just know" creates an atmosphere of insecurity instead of team cohesiveness.
- Employee feedback offers key input to owners and managers and encourages everyone to work in the best interests of the business. They make great sounding boards.
- Higher staff turnover and low morale are often the results of poor accountability. The net effect can be milestones/performance targets not met, and a general "who really cares" malaise that blights the business environment.

Governance

We all live by rules which govern us. Business is no different.

- A clear division of responsibility makes everyone in the company aware of their role, and that of their associates.
- Corporate policies and procedures clearly state what acceptable behavior is and what the company's position is on numerous matters. That includes vacations, bonuses, sick days, and pay scales for specific job responsibilities and length of service. Inconsistent policy enforcement negates the value and merit of even having those policies in place.

- An organigram helps employees and managers understand who each person reports to. These lines of reporting are critical pathways in maintaining order and responsibility.
- Governance applies equally to the company's Board and Directors.
    - Risk management control and monitoring, and acting on any situation that compromises the company's financial well-being and threatens its asset base.
    - A primary function of a Board is oversight. Neglecting or marginalizing oversight can certainly cost the company opportunities.

The client was a new cosmetics company with an extensive line of all-natural products. Its mix was timely. The market need was proven. Its brand was quickly becoming a rage with consumers. And its management was struggling to keep up.

To their credit, they recognized that they were on a collision course. Their shortcomings were sure to catch up with them.

- Virtually no structured management. It was more of a free-for-all with everyone doing as much as they could, but nobody was really responsible for monitoring or tracking their vital and often sporadic supply chain.
- Delays in billing and in the collection of receivables were causing a serious cash crunch.
- Where mistakes were being made, there was nobody from the top down embracing them. Corrective action was not a learning experience, but a scramble to do a quick fix and move on.
- Financial planning was limited to checking the bank balance. When additional funds to handle the rapid growth of the company were needed, the company was ill-prepared to meet with funders.

The business was in full growth, but their troubles were heart breaking.

- Our first task was to generate a Business Plan both for the use of the company management and for presentation to funders.

- We helped them secure funding, which alleviated some pressures.
- Next, we dealt with two priorities: invoicing and collections.
- Our ensuing area of involvement was helping to design divisions of responsibility for each of their people and establishing a reporting hierarchy structure.
- Finally, we recommended management training for their founders and executives to augment their skills in dealing with issues, tracking performance, and setting goals and expectations for the business and for their staff.

Score	Good Mistake Rating	Bad Mistake Rating	Ugly Mistake Rating
3			
2			
1			

Lesson(s) Learned: When a business grows exponentially, many consider it a good thing, and it is, except for the mayhem it causes. Opportunities are replaced with challenges with which to cope. Direction and growth are often set aside to deliver on what was overpromised. The solution is taking a step back, or engaging a third party to do so, and dealing with priorities. Providing some breathing room for management is key.

The company learned that growth in itself creates problems, from funding to handling bottlenecks and challenges, many of which can inflict pain. Their learning/acceptance process was slow as they let problems slide. When the situation became critical, the owners finally undertook action to parallel their business to fit their changing needs. The mandate was a multifold challenge, earning this instance a "2" in the Bad | Mistakes Rating. Their delay in responding could have proved fatal.

SECTION FOUR

Fixing the Fixables and Moving On

Section Four presents a discussion on fixable mistakes that you can and should learn from, a "Let's Deal with It" checklist that can help you track the advent and impact of mistakes, and a brief discussion on founder exit strategies, the entrepreneur's daydream of an ultimate payback/reward.

As well, Section Four offers counsel on how to predict business errors before they happen, and optimizing corporate culture.

There is also a chapter on yet more real-world stories/case studies of situations that reflect mistakes that have made us proud to have resolved, as well as those for which we may have shed a tear of sorrow, or laughter.

CHAPTER 29

Fixing the Fixables

"Mistakes are the growing pains of WISDOM."

—William George Jordan

Fixing mistakes has certain unshakable truisms. They are simple and straightforward, but only if you accept their veracity. Here they are.

1. Most mistakes are fixable, especially if caught and dealt with before irreversible damage is done. Mistakes need to be recognized and embraced.
2. Mistakes are not your enemy unless you let them fester unchallenged.
3. You cannot fix it when you surround yourself with people who fear bringing mistakes to your attention. Fear is an ally of mistakes.
4. If you cannot capitalize on a mistake, then you have missed an opportunity.
5. Pain avoidance is not a strategy to deal with mistakes. It only makes it worse.
6. If everything in your business is working well, get suspicious. There may be "mistakes in waiting" that can be resolved more easily in their infancy.
7. If you cannot fix it, hire someone who can. Expertise is rentable.
8. If mistakes are impacting your health or stealing your sleep, or upsetting your work–life balance, then you have waited too long to initiate action. Time to attack and resolve the issue(s).
9. Trust your instincts to recognize issues and take remedial action. You are, after all, likely the one responsible for safeguarding the business you have striven to build. Problem solving starts at the top.

The "Let's Deal with It" Process

There is a process for identifying mistakes, embracing them, gauging their ability to harm, reigning them in, and learning to capitalize on them. Here is a **checklist**.

The Mistake	How Have You Dealt with It?
How did you recognize the mistake?	
At what point has the issue become recognizable as a threat?	
Have you assessed the potential impact?	
What gap or loophole in your infrastructure or organization allowed the mistake to happen?	
Is this a recurrence or a new error?	
If it is a recurrence, how was it resolved before, and did you establish a roadblock to assure it does not happen again?	
Who in your organization is the "ground zero" originator? This isn't laying blame; it is an effort to identify how the mistake manifested itself.	
Was it caught early, or did it fester to the point of urgency?	
Has the business incurred a financial loss? If yes, what value have you assigned the loss?	
Will this impact on your reputation in the marketplace? If yes, how will you deal with it?	
Has your customer base been affected? If yes, how will you communicate with your clients and address their concerns?	
What is the potential fix? Mitigating strategy?	
Do you need to engage an outside third party to add resources necessary to design or provide a fix?	
Will this require a rethink in your staffing, management team, internal division of responsibility or lines of authority?	
What have you learned from the mistake?	
Has it provided a positive impact for you such as greater IP protection, implementation of a rapid mistake identification process, a new opportunity that was birthed from the mistake? Anything else?	
In hindsight, how could the mistake have been avoided or averted?	

Zombie Mistakes

Often referred to as potential "business killers," this category of mistakes can be fatal and need to be dealt with ruthlessly as soon as they are detected.

- A convergence of missteps, where any number of mistakes from different sources within your business come together to form "the perfect storm." An example might be a competitor releasing new technology and your company being ill-prepared to leapfrog it because you have lost (and not replaced) your key innovators, or it is impossible to build on your existing products or platform.
- You know something is amiss but cannot identify all of its source(s) or impact. It's akin to waiting for the serpent to strike. It creates anxiety and distress in the process, but you are at a loss how to intervene.
- Silent unmonitored killers, such as diminishing product demand, economic downturns, skyrocketing burn rates where harnessing spending will have serious growth impact, unforeseen delays in product/service launches or stagnation, or an inability or disinterest to change.
- Growing debt, which brings with it higher interest costs and possibly prohibitive alternate funding sources and detrimental terms and conditions. This also can imply taking on "vulture debt" where any missed performance milestone can trigger financial penalties or relinquishing a portion of your shares.
- Year after year declines in your company performance which are difficult to clearly pinpoint or source because issues overlap. Fixing one blunder exacerbates others lurking behind it.
- Obstinance implies relying on outdated Business Plans, old historical financials (when things were better for your company), or rigid market strategies in an ever-changing marketplace.

Fixable Mistakes You Can Learn the Most From

Mistakes in any of these strategically important areas can deliver the most impactful learning experiences and opportunities, both for your business and for you.

- Not securing sufficient working capital, as well as capital acquisition funding.
- Underspending on marketing.
- Ignoring customer satisfaction, a key to developing customer and brand loyalty.
- Ignoring feedback from those who support your business, namely customers and your team of managers and staff.
- Marketing that is inconsistent, poorly delivered and has no call to action. It just "is."
- Assuming good cash flow goes on indefinitely. It does not. Action needs to be taken to monitor and control cash flow.
- Relying on third-hand information, i.e., "I heard at the luncheon that ..."
- Hiring who you like instead of who you need. That includes hiring family and friends who might be impossible to de-hire and may be less competent too.
- Failure to recognize opportunities, possibly out of complacency, which can be yet another business killer.
- Inability or unwillingness to adapt when those around you, including competitors, are doing so. Remaining the "odd duck" is not conducive for you maintaining and growing your market share.

Zombie mistakes are ugly.

These **recommendations** deal primarily with bettering yourself and making you more decisive, capable of strategic planning and decision making without second-guessing yourself and assuring that you confront brewing mistakes with results-oriented determination.

- Mindfulness instills caution and astute awareness with your surroundings. Practice it.
- Change "fear to act" to "fear not to act."
- Learn to pivot and adapt to whatever circumstances you come face-to-face with.

- Fix things so you can have the time, resources, and flexibility to grow things.
- Refocus on your goals to reflect where you want to be and not where you came from.
- Learn from everything that goes on around you, every hiccup, every near disaster. Mistakes are great teachers and often open pathways to change and new opportunities.
- Take pride in your abilities. Build on your achievements and your strengths.
- Refill your entrepreneurship resource toolbox after every mistake you overcome. Chances are you may need to draw from your experience next time you confront a new challenge.
- Finally, think about engaging a Business Consultant who can provide unfettered, objective advice and solutions that you may not be able to see.

CHAPTER 30

Reading the Tea Leaves: Predicting Mistakes

> *"The greatest mistake you can make in life is to be continually fearing you will make one."*
>
> —Elbert Hubbard

If you can predict the next pending blunder, you will have created a less disruptive environment for your people, able to devote more of your time to forward-thinking instead of dealing with adversities, and, overall, allowing yourself and your team to focus on the innovative and exciting instead of continually putting out fires.

Predicting and avoiding mistakes enhances your abilities as an entrepreneur/manager and increases your personal and professional capital.

Is this simply wishful thinking? No. There are **markers** *or* **indicators** *that should tweak your "Danger, Will Robinson" warning signal.*[12] *Here are the most formative markers.*

- The most blatant trends that signify problems and/or mistakes are cash flow issues, declining gross margins and declining sales, either overall revenues or sales of specific products or services. These are the easiest factors for you to continuously monitor.
- Related to the above, there can be a loss of market share and loyal customers, both of which trends can be effectively monitored.

[12]Robby the Robot is a fictional character who first appeared in the 1956 film *Forbidden Planet,* then in *Lost in Space.* He coined the famous line "Danger, Will Robinson, Danger!" and … has the distinction as "the hardest working robot in Hollywood"—"Robby the Robot," Wikipedia, https://en.wikipedia.org/wiki/Robby_the_Robot.

- Burgeoning expenses without any visible payback tells a story of decision-making problems. Every expenditure needs to add real and realizable value to the business.
- Climbing debt that does not correspond to the need to finance growing accounts receivable or expanding the best turnover inventories. This may also indicate a decline in your "accounts receivable turnover/days sales outstanding," which may be yet another marker of problems intensifying.
- Dead/slow moving inventory that may need to be disposed of at a loss. This also indicates issues with your purchasing policies or dissociation with current market trends.
- Major mistakes are highly visible. However, a constant flow of minor problems, especially repeating problems cropping up, even when they are effectively resolved, steal time and focus away from you and your staff and managers.
- High employee turnover indicates a level of dissatisfaction among your staff. Even more damaging is high turnover of managers and key people you rely on.
- Customer complaints or staff suggestions being ignored are indicative of poor leadership skills.

My client, a service provider, experienced full growth, to the extent that, even with hiring new staff, there was a constant stream of problems. Many were caused by newbies, or staff responsibilities constantly being shifted to accommodate the rapid development of the venture, or gaps in training and orientation.

Problems were inherently part of the business.

This was now extending to negative customer feedback, which was the trigger in their reaching out to me for help.

It had gotten to the point that the founders spent more time extinguishing fires than they did actually running the business. I was surprised how consuming this was for the owners, not being able to focus on the successful machine they had built. They were struggling to keep everything on an even keel but really failing to do so.

After a close (and exhausting) review of their internal structure, division of responsibility and critical communications, including customer input, my solution was implementing Occam's Razor[13] that teaches the best solution to a problem is usually the simplest one.

I encouraged them to hire a manager whose role was to maintain objectivity, observe all key aspects of the company's operation among and between the team as well as dealings with customer issues and corporate policy, and suggest changes to alleviate the problems. This was also intended to free up more time for the founders who were being buried and burned.

The new position was titled "Pre-Problem Solver." This move was welcomed by the staff and worked as an effective firewall between the founders and the problems/mistakes. It worked wonders.

Score	Good Mistake Rating	Bad Mistake Rating	Ugly Mistake Rating
3			
2			
1			

Lesson(s) Learned: Simple solutions work, particularly where there is a plethora of small bonfires that are occupying too much time for the staff and owners. The key is to deal with the foundations of often-recurring mistakes and provide a comfort zone for all the business's people to simply do their jobs. Occam's Razor often prevails.

Where practical, simple solutions with a hint of innovation deliver concrete results, the net effect will always be a high score in the ratings chart. In this instance, a solid good ratings of "3" was well deserved.

[13]"Occam's razor," Wikipedia, https://en.wikipedia.org/wiki/Occam%27s_razor.

CHAPTER 31

Punitive Versus Blameless Business Culture

"Company culture is the backbone of any successful organization."
—Gary Vaynerchuk

A punitive corporate culture that prefers to lay blame for mistakes is extremely counterproductive. It encourages the cover-up of blunders, stifles innovative thinking, negatively impacts on motivation, reduces expectations, diminishes respect for leadership, instills an atmosphere of fear of retribution, and, most importantly, can dramatically shrink the company's capital.

That's a lot of negative food for thought.

The other side of the equation, a blameless culture, builds on respect, embracing errors without fear of being judged or punished, and focuses on a future where errors are dealt with and rarely repeated. That behavior adds to the personal and professional growth of everyone, from the top down.

So why is a punitive culture so prevalent? Because the "punishers" are weak, insecure managers and poor leaders.

Conversely, those spearheading a blameless culture are more prone to turn mistakes into motivation, embracing rather than finger-pointing. Understanding and being compassionate instead of being small-minded and ego driven.

Here are some key differences between the two philosophies.

Characteristic	Punitive	Blameless
Governing intent	Finding someone to blame. Often anyone.	Work to identify the source in order to prevent its repetition and fill any evident gaps.
Focus	Punishment	Learn from mistakes and grow

(continued)

Characteristic	Punitive	Blameless
Employees	Instill fear, apprehension, stifling performance, and motivation	Feeling safe, protected, and committed to their responsibilities, mistake-free wherever feasible
Ego	Mistakes are others' responsibility, important to lay blame and make others "pay"	Able to embrace and move on without being ego driven
Outcome	Staff turnover, resistance to taking direction, insecurity, poor job performance	Employees and management constantly striving to improve
Capital	An attitude that stifles capital. In a punitive framework, mistakes are not seen as a learning experience, but as a reason for punishment.	Welcomes learning from past blunders and provide a resource for your toolbox. Create a better manager or entrepreneur and staff.

One of my early career CEOs was a "hound." By that I mean he was abusive to everyone beneath him, except for the "secretary of the month's revolving door" with whom he would carry on a fling. He discouraged free thought and was entirely self-centered and ego driven.

He was the epitome of a punitive culture leader whose leadership skills revolved around, "If it works, I did it. If it backfires, tag, you're it."

How could the company survive? It couldn't.

Despite forming a committee in which I participated and all of us offering a number of suggestions and action planning to steer the company toward a blameless culture, everything we recommended was dismissed offhandedly by him.

When the business finally succumbed, I helped negotiate an employee buyout and secured government funding to facilitate the transition. It worked.

Once that was done, I had little impetus to stay on. The scars were far too fresh.

Score	Good Mistake Rating	Bad Mistake Rating	Ugly Mistake Rating
3			
2			
1			

Lesson(s) Learned: My suggestion is that if and when you find yourself in an abusive culture, realize that your future advancement is likely limited, unless you yourself become a clone of the punitive creator-in-charge.

Ugly mistakes, even when tempered by corrective action, generally remain ugly. The issues that brought about the need for change eventually returned and the business backslid into chaos. A "3" in the "Ugly Mistake Rating" category was well-earned.

CHAPTER 32

Pivoting Your Business Away from Making Mistakes

"Pivoting is not the end of the disruption process, but the beginning of the next leg of your journey."

—Jay Samit

At some point you may arrive at the decision that you need to make a dramatic shift in your business. The business model you have been following over the last 10 years is just not working. Possibly the market has shifted dramatically while you have remained motionless. Some of your products or services have become outdated, or obsolete. You have been leery about entering social media/online commerce because you have no understanding of it, and a reticence to even learn.

Regardless, you are at a junction in your business. Change dramatically or die.

Pivoting is radical change, but what does it imply? Just how is it carried out?

The act of pivoting can represent a new beginning, a learning event, a distinct asset in both your own capital, and an increase in the value of your business.

Here in a nutshell are the stages in pivoting.

1. Understand your marketplace and where you stand amid your competitors.
2. Carry out a host of KPIs (see earlier chapter in this book) to determine the health of your business.
3. Is your business model still viable? Find out.
4. Get as much feedback from customers and staff. Where and how might you change to serve everyone better? Learn to listen.

5. Carry out research and feasibility studies on any ideas and suggestions that appear to have some merit. Think about innovation.
6. Profile your ideal customer. Has your customer base changed/shifted? Can you appeal to any new client base?
7. Assess the relevance of your current products and services. Still timely? Serving the needs of the customers?
8. Review your supply chains to determine if you are getting value and service.
9. Is your marketing strategy working? Run tests and focus groups and surveys to find out.
10. Create a Pivoting Action Plan, preferably in small, controllable "baby steps."
11. Your clients, funders, distributors, suppliers, and staff all need to be apprised of your pivoting strategy. They will be important players in the process.

We were mandated to establish new supply chains for titanium bicycle parts with a major overseas Third World supplier. We followed through and set up a series of face-to-face meetings to launch the discussions.

My clients' costs, margins, and production schedules were based on building this new relationship. This was critical. Goodwill payments were already made.

To our surprise, dealing with the overseas manufacturer was hell.

- They were uncertain of a steady supply of titanium, and the prices fluctuated wildly with no warning.
- They contracted out a fair amount of production and could not guarantee adherence to any reasonable schedule or quality control standards.
- Their export department was lax and amateurish, with little knowledge of dealing with overseas customers, and the mass of paperwork and permitting that required.

Our client was adamant about salvaging the relationship.
A Pivoting Action Plan was more of a survival plan.

- We became the lead in the contract.
- We engaged a western-style production and engineering firm with offices near the suppliers' plant.
- We designed a training program for the supplier's production people and export department. We instilled western concepts including quality control, timelines, and timely deliveries.
- We became a natural extension of the supplier's operation.

Score	Good Mistake Rating	Bad Mistake Rating	Ugly Mistake Rating
3			
2			
1			

Lesson(s) Learned: Pivoting is an important business tool. It resolves issues, sets new pathways, mends relationships, and focus forward, not mired in hindsight. In regards to the case study discussed above, the new relationship between willing partners generated better communication, doable delivery schedules, and, where necessary, training for the supplier's management. Without significant pivoting, the opportunity to work together would have been lost.

This was not a liaison built on trust. The fallout from the mistake of trying to build a working relationship was exacerbated by the fact that our client badly needed the foreign supplier, and the supplier was keenly aware of it. Our client had painted themselves into a corner. New sources of supply should have been sought much earlier, before damages were incurred. Extricating them was doable, but there was a price to pay. The relationship with the foreign supplier deteriorated over several more years. Luckily, on our advice, our client had built new avenues for material, a little late, but functional nonetheless. Still, a "2" on the "Ugly Mistake Chart" was warranted.

CHAPTER 33
Cashing Out

"Don't be afraid to give up the good to go for the great."
—John D. Rockefeller

My philosophy on business is that you build it to sell it. That is the upside return on your investment, efforts, commitments, and growth. You cash out.

Every business I launched as a dedicated "start-up junkie" was born with that eventual exit strategy in mind.

Every opportunity for growth, change, expansion, acquisition, significant partnership, and new market development had that very end goal in mind. Build it and sell it. It is still my priority strategy.

Having said that, there are many exit ramps, as depicted herein. Your ultimate selection is based on seeking out the best returns, the circumstances of the sale, the deal, and your comfort level pertaining to the exit strategies you wish to pursue.

The choice is yours. The end result is always cashing out. Here are a few avenues to consider.

Sale of the business. This is the most often chosen course of action. The process is to find a willing player, often a competitor, and commissioning a valuation as a starting point. Valuations are somewhat of a black art, with different models yielding different net worth. It is highly advisable to contract your own valuation and compare results with the prospective buyer.[14]

[14]"Valuations are a useful tool when buying or selling your business or negotiating with an investor or partner. However, it is a 'black art.' There are various valuation methodologies, and the outcomes can differ tremendously. Valuations are driven by self-interest, so beware. Multiples of revenues and EBITDA used in valuations are generally cited as a range, with buyers using the lowest multiples and sellers using the highest. A valuation done by a buyer will definitely not be the same as one done by a seller."—Jay Silverberg, A Cynic's Business Wisdom: Winning ThroughFlexible Ethics(Business Expert Press, 2021).

The process of selling your business follows a pattern of events and undertakings by both parties. An excellent synopsis on when and how to sell your business is available online on various websites.

Succession involves leaving the business to a child, or possibly a relative. This is a common strategy, but only really works if the recipient has had hands-on experience in the company and is comfortable taking on the reigns of leadership. My favorite case study is a client of a very profitable company where the owner handed over the business to his nephew who had spent 15 years working his way up the ranks from inventory clerk to Vice President. Further, the nephew's father had previously handed the business over to the current owner who was simply "paying it forward." It was a heartfelt scenario to witness.

Management buyouts or employee ownership plans ensure that those who become the new owners have the inherent experience and motivation to carry on and succeed. However, the legalities can be off-putting.

Public offering. While his strategy is time-consuming and fraught with legal and regulatory hurdles, the financial returns can be significant. The dark horse is that quite often the founders' shares have a hold on them for a period of time and the hope is that the business survives and grows during that interim hold period until the shares can be sold.

Lesson(s) Learned: Everything I did from the day I planned and opened my consulting practice was geared toward building my business and selling it downstream.

- Selected a "power" name and developed a memorable brand and branding vision statement
- Rented impressive but limited space with a large corner window office for me to impress clients
- Hired my team based on credentials, the universities they graduated from, and their resume of recognizable past accomplishments
- Worked to maintain a high success rate by being selective in the contracts I accepted

- Performed pro bono work to enhance my firm's visibility
- Took on speaking engagements at conferences and workshops, including as a guest speaker invited to university business courses
- Built a close liaison with media and benefited from public exposure
- Determined when my business was peaking as the target for selling
- Engaged an independent third-party business valuation company, but, since I was paying their bills, any valuation they prepared were likely to benefit me
- Prepared a shortlist of prospective buyers
- Negotiated as if I did not need to sell with a foregone conclusion in my mind that I was selling, which I did

CHAPTER 34

More Business Adventures, Tales, Triumphs, and Trouble

"Launching a business is essentially an adventure in problem-solving."
—Richard Branson

Community Economic Drivers Identified

A large community was in the midst of developing an investor attraction presentation for use at a global summit in Japan. What they needed was hard evidence of the economic drivers that were generating jobs and opportunities, something they could use as proof the region was a worthwhile investment target.

We went about our mandate interviewing community leaders, pouring over economic data and activity that could be classified as key sectors driving the economy.

This was a resource community that hosted significant employers, and, as such, it was generally assumed that our results would confirm this preconceived scenario.

Upon completing our work, we reported to the mayor and regional representatives. Our results were painful beyond question.

The major economic driver was an underground cannabis economy. Estimates of employment, exports, and economic stability were clearly in favor of cannabis growers, harvesters, and exporters.

We were curtly terminated, and yet our findings were conclusive and upheld by hard data.

The community reoriented their investment presentation before attending the conference. Cannabis was not mentioned.

Lesson(s) Learned: Any and all market research needs to be impartial and strives to deliver facts, not fiction. When the client has preconceived ideas, that is an invitation for pending conflict.

Killer B Tees

This was one of our fun contracts. The client had secured the licensing rights to a number of retro movie posters and heroes: *Flash Gordon*, *Radar Men from the Moon*, *The Masked Avenger*, *Space Captain*, *Emperor Mongo*, *Captain Video*, and many more.

The name Killer B Tees makes reference to the hundreds of B movies and serial cliffhangers produced on shoestring budgets in the 1930s and the 1940s and even 1950s, and shown weekly at movie houses well into the 1960s, attracting an audience each week to catch up on their heroes, their exploits, and their near-death escapes. And, of course, their relentless fight to protect the American dream. By modern media standards, they were clumsy and campy but highly entertaining.

We were asked to help develop an inexpensive but effective product launch campaign.

We rose to the challenge by suggesting a guerilla marketing campaign. Superheroes and villains, in full costume, were sent out to wander the major streets and districts that housed offices, restaurants, bars, and other assorted watering holes.

We then invited the media to take in the splashy, noisy launch. It was estimated that Killer B Tees received free advertising and exposure valued in the hundreds of thousands. Dealers and distributors vied for distribution rights and online sales.

My team and I had enough Killer B Tees to last us years that never failed to draw attention.

Lesson(s) Learned: Marketing often demands a creative and imaginative approach, including guerilla marketing as an effective option to consider. The expression "stepping out of the box" rarely carried more meaning than the Killer B Tees campaign.

Pedicab Distress

A company was launching a pedicab tourist service to offer city tours to cruise passengers. The city was a stop for numerous cruise ships heading up to Alaska or over to Hawaii.

Within a short period of operation, the company was undergoing constant driver turnover to the point that a large number of pedicabs were sitting idle.

It was determined, after interviewing ex-drivers, that the attractions catering to tourists were quite hilly, and the summer heat, in conjunction with portly cruise ship tourists, was too much of a burden for the drivers.

We offered three solutions; switch to motorized Tuk Tuks (motorized pedicabs) imported from Viet Nam, Thailand, and Cambodia, charge more for the tours, and increase the wages to the operators, including a bonus based on the number of tours they booked.

Lesson(s) Learned: Business solutions are not always complicated, but outside experts tend to look at issues more objectively and offer solutions often overlooked by the company itself. Remember Occam's Razor.

Appendix: A Mistake by Any Other Name Is Still a Mistake[15]

"A mistake repeated more than once is a decision."
—Paulo Coelho, Author

Throughout this book we have endeavored to substitute the word "mistake" for other terms, just to limit excessive repetition. Blunders, gaffes, miscues, missteps, and errors, among others, have frequented the chapters herein. The optional expressions are listed below.

"You make mistakes. Mistakes don't make you."[16]

The successful businessperson needs to walk the fine line between avoiding day-to-day management and operational mistakes versus capitalizing on potential opportunities by taking a leap, which can ultimately be a mistake in itself.

Nobody ever claimed business was simple.

Strongest matches

- aberration
- blunder
- confusion
- fault
- gaffe
- inaccuracy
- lapse

Strong matches

- blooper
- boo-boo
- bungle
- delusion
- erratum
- flub
- fluff
- muddle
- neglect
- overestimation
- slight
- slip
- solecism
- trip
- underestimation

---

[15]"Mistake," ***Thesaurus.com***, https://www.thesaurus.com/browse/mistake.
[16]Maxwell Maltz, *Psycho-Cybernetics* (Pocket Books, 1960).

- miscalculation
- misconception
- misstep
- omission
- oversight
- snafu
- flaw
- illusion
- inadvertence
- misapplication
- misapprehension
- misinterpretation
- misprint
- misstatement

Weak matches

- false move
- false step
- faux pas
- misjudgment

About the Author

Jay J. Silverberg (BA Honors Psychology and Bachelor of Commerce) is a "business rebel" who has started and run a number of successful businesses.

This book is a culmination of his business adventures (and misadventures) and offers up a multitude of inestimably valuable lessons.

As an entrepreneurial trainer, Jay has developed innovative programs for both the beginner and the advanced businessperson, and delivered training and mentoring to thousands of entrepreneurs, managers, and business professionals.

As a business consultant, Jay's practice ranges from start-ups to Fortune 500 firms with projects that have spanned the globe. He has also represented government, trade, and economic development ministries at national and international conferences.

Jay Silverberg currently teaches entrepreneurship and delivers business coaching and mentoring. *Mistakes Are Your Capital* is Jay's sixth Business Expert Press book on entrepreneurship, mentoring, and training. Please visit https://www.businessexpertpress.com/?s=Jay+J+Silverberg

Jay resides near Vancouver, British Columbia, Canada with his wife, Linda, who inspires him to always see life as a gift, and business as a game (and vice versa).

Jay can be contacted at jssynergy@gmail.com

Other Books by Jay J. Silverberg

Silverberg, Jay J. 2021. *A Cynic's Business Wisdom: Winning Through Flexible Ethics.* Business Express Press.

Silverberg, Jay J., and Bruce E. McLean. 2022. *Dead Fish Don't Swim Upstream: Real Life Lessons in Entrepreneurship.* Business Express Press.

Silverberg, Jay J. 2023. *Stuck Entrepreneurs: Escape Routes Out of the Quicksand.* Business Express Press.

Silverberg, Jay J. 2024. *The Start-Up Junkie's Playbook: A 30-Step Plan to Launch Your Business.* Business Express Press.

Silverberg, Jay J. 2025. *Powerhouse Business Mentorship: A How-To Handbook for Mentors and Mentees.* Business Express Press.

Acknowledgment

On a personal note…

Mistakes Are Your Capital is my sixth book in the entrepreneurial mentoring series. **It is now part of my collection, "The Synergy of Being in Business."**

After book number five, *Powerhouse Business Mentorship*, I was convinced that I had come to the end of my authoring journey, and yet, here I am again.

This will be it. Everything I have learned or experienced in business is now recorded, in print and digitally. My cluttered business brain is now empty.

Aside from the usual dedications to wife and family, I would like to extend my appreciation to Scott Isenberg and Scott Shane of Business Expert Press, who have supported and encouraged me, and, with "an iron fist in a velvet glove," redirected me when I wandered off the trail, and did so kindly and caringly. Thank you.

Jay J. Silverberg
May, 2026

"On and on you will hike.
And I know you'll hike far
and face up to your problems
whatever they are."

—Dr. Seuss

Index

www.ingramcontent.com/pod-product-compliance
Lightning Source LLC
LaVergne TN
LVHW050630100826
845148LV00011B/1811

9781606495711